DILBERT™ AND THE WAY OF THE WEASEL

Also by Scott Adams

The Dilbert Principle
Dogbert's Top Secret Management Handbook
The Dilbert Future
The Joy of Work

DILBERT™ AND THE
WAY OF THE WEASEL

SCOTT ADAMS

B🌱XTREE

First published 2002 by HarperCollins, New York

This edition published 2002 by Boxtree
an imprint of Pan Macmillan Ltd
20 New Wharf Road, London N1 9RR
Basingstoke and Oxford
Associated companies throughout the world

www.panmacmillan.com

ISBN 0 7522 6503 2

135798642

A CIP catalogue record for this book is available from
the British Library.

Printed by Mackays of Chatham plc

For my favorite weasel

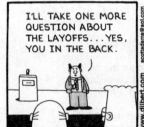
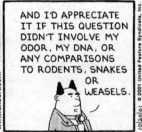
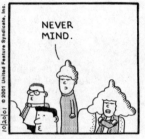

To err is human.
To cover it up is weasel.

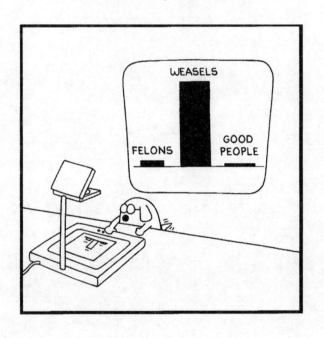

Contents

Contents

DILBERT™ AND THE
WAY OF THE WEASEL

Introduction

In my previous scholarly book, *The Dilbert Principle,* I explained my theory that idiots are systematically identified and promoted to management. That book is now required reading at a number of colleges and universities.*

Being an author and all, I had been enjoying my role as a member of the intelligentsia (God, I hope I spelled that right), but I had a nagging feeling that my theory was incomplete. In case you have been frittering away your life by not reading Dilbert books, I will summarize the 300+ pages of *The Dilbert Principle* so you can judge for yourself.

The Dilbert Principle *Summarized*

A retarded chimpanzee can drink a case of beer and still perform most management functions.

If that seems harsh, look at this list of management functions and figure out which ones the chimp couldn't do.

*If you'd like a list of those schools so you can avoid them, send a self-addressed, stamped envelope to someone who has that information.

Management Functions

- Avoiding decisions
- Attending meetings
- Babbling
- Demanding status reports
- Not reading status reports
- Handing out random rewards and punishments
- Scowling at people who believe the Open Door Policy

Your first reaction might be that the Dilbert Principle is so comprehensive that there is no room left for any other ideas in the world and so you might as well roll up in a ball and die. I thought the same thing. But over time I became more certain that my theory was incomplete. I racked my brain* and came up with a new and improved theory that explains not just management but, dare I say, humanity.

New Improved Theory

People are weasels.

When I say "weasels," I'm sure you know what I mean. But that won't stop me from explaining it for a few hundred more pages

---

*After I racked my brain, I chalked my nose.

because it's the sort of thoroughness that you expect from a member of the intelligencia, or innteligentia, or whatever.

I shall start with an example of weaselness.

Weasel Example

At some point in your career you will be asked to train a new person to take over your job. It would be embarrassing if your coworkers found out that your job can be learned in two hours. You've spent an entire career convincing people that what you do is slightly harder than performing brain surgery with chopsticks.

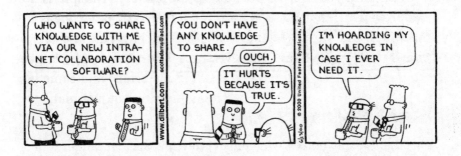

That's why, as a weasel, you want to leave out vital information during the training. It's a delicate balance. You need to instill in your trainee a feeling that he or she knows how to do the job while having no actual competence. Ideally you want your trainee to make an embarrassing and costly mistake right out of the gate so people will long for the good old days of you.

Every job has some vital yet nonobvious component that can be left out of the training without your trainee (victim) being the wiser. When your trainee is humiliated by your deception and threatening to attack you, slap your forehead and proclaim your guilt for not mentioning that *one* important thing in the training. Try not to laugh or pump your fist or dance a jig.

As your final gesture of badwill, before you leave, hand your replacement a file and claim with a straight face, "Everything you need to know is in this file." Ideally the file will be bits of candy wrappers and keyboard lint that you've been accumulating for years.

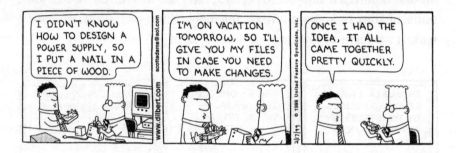

Weasel Definitions

Throughout this book I will concoct new phrases and definitions so that my ideas are revolutionary. As you know, nothing worth knowing can be explained with regular words.

Weasel Zone: There's a gigantic gray area between good moral behavior and outright felonious activities. I call that the *Weasel Zone** and it's where most of life happens.

*Sometimes also known as Weaselville, Weaseltown, the Way of the Weasel, Weaselopolis, Weaselburg, and Redmond.

In the Weasel Zone everything is misleading, but not *exactly* a lie. There's a subtle difference. When you lie, you hope to fool someone. But when you're being a weasel, everyone is aware that you're a manipulative, scheming, misleading sociopath. For example, no one believes an engineer who says he's going to explain something briefly. No one believes a contractor who says the job will be done in a week. No one believes a salesperson who says there are no hidden costs. No one believes a politician who says large contributors don't influence his decisions. And no one believes a lawyer who says, "Have a nice day." You know none of that is sincere. And *they* know that *you* know, so in a way, it's a form of honesty—a weasel form.

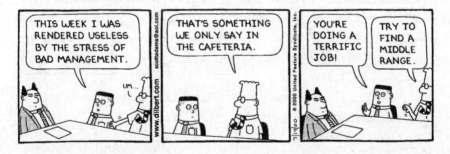

Weaselness is everywhere. Here's a fresh example that was reported to me by e-mail while I was writing this introduction:

Situation: A company full of raging weasels keeps its field service people on their toes by making them track how long it takes to fix customer problems. A particular customer made a complaint and waited *two years* before anyone was even assigned to work on the problem.

Now, given the level of weasel saturation in the company,

how do you think the service department tracked their perform-ance for that customer?

Option 1: Did they report each week to their bosses—for two years—that they were incompetent?

Or

Option 2: Did they log the customer's problem into the tracking system on the same day someone was finally assigned to fix it—two years after the original complaint—thus showing an excel-lent response record?

The first method is totally honest; it shows the service department for what it is: uncaring and incompetent. The sec-ond method—the Way of the Weasel—keeps everyone employed and has the added advantage of training the customer not to complain anymore.

Answer: The customer had weasel footprints up one side of her and down the other.

If you are honest and ethical in the traditional—i.e., non-weasel–way, then people will respect you. They'll also steal everything you own because honest people never see it coming. If you want to be safe from weasels, you need to think like a weasel. I recommend maintaining a constant level of mistrust and cynicism that is almost—but not quite—enough to qualify you for involuntary institutionalization.

There's a fine line between healthy mistrust of humanity and outright paranoia. It's perfectly okay to *think* that Microsoft is cloning huge attack dogs to further its goal of total global domi-nation, but you don't want to say it out loud. Then, when the dogs attack, and you're the only one wearing Kevlar underpants, you'll have the last laugh.

If you're not experienced at being distrustful, I recommend starting with something easy: make a list of all the things your parents told you when you were young, e.g., Easter bunny, Santa Claus, tooth fairy, coins growing in your ears, suspicious causes of blindness. From there it's a short hop to this.

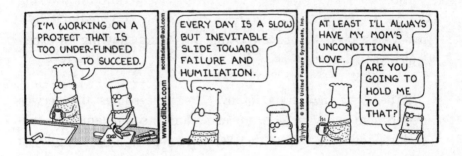

After you have mastered complete mistrust of your immediate family, it's time to extend your paranoia to coworkers and your boss. Again you want to curb your instinct to say out loud any honest thoughts. Here are some examples of traditional honest behavior that inhabitants of the Weasel Zone should avoid.

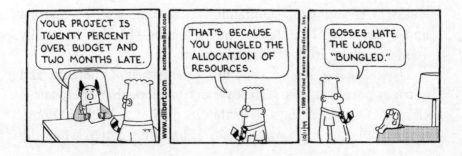

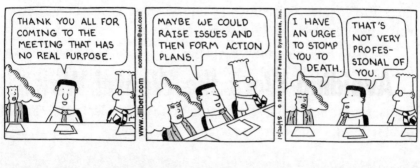

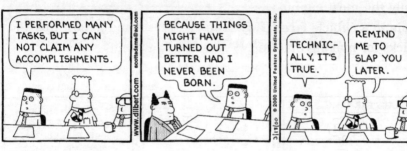

1

Avoiding Work the Weasel Way

Only the most cunning weasels can survive thirty years of hard time in a cubicle farm. This chapter offers some weasel tips and tricks for making that thirty years feel like twenty-nine.

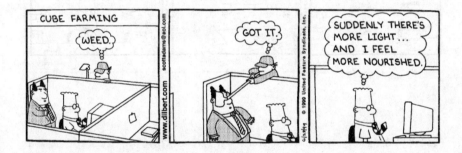

Overcommitting

For every task you plan to do, it's a good idea to have sixty tasks that you've promised to do later if you ever find the time. This gives everyone the impression that you are valiantly battling an avalanche of work and fighting against long odds to make the company successful. Or they might just think you're a worthless, inefficient weasel. Either way, the pay is exactly the same and it cuts down on your workload.

The Long Run

The great thing about the "long run" is that it's someone else's problem, especially when it comes to things like corporate disaster planning. As a weasel employee, your personal disaster-recovery plan is to drive across town and get a job at a place that didn't have a disaster. In the meantime, there's no benefit to you in fighting for a budget for some thankless task like backing up computer files.

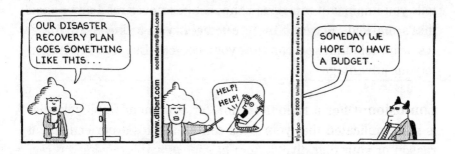

Compliance

Have you ever noticed that the word *complying* has the word *lying* built right into it? That's probably not a coincidence.

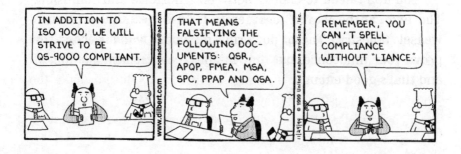

Given a choice between complying with a ridiculous policy and *pretending* to comply, weasels will do whatever is easiest. Usually it's easiest to pretend. If you choose to pretend, then you need an escape plan in case you get caught. Here are the most common defenses for noncomplying weasels:

Ignorance: Ignorance is no excuse for breaking the law. But when it comes to your job, ignorance is an excellent excuse because it's so believable. Between the fact that your boss never tells you important things and the fact you never read any e-mail that's marked "urgent," no one expects you to know anything. It's a miracle that you can find your cubicle. Use that reputation to your advantage.

Confusion: Offer a rationalization for your noncompliance that is so complicated that your boss can't tell if it's a perfectly good reason or your digestive system has inexplicably reversed directions. Pile the buzzwords high and deep. The average person can only understand a sentence that has up to three acronyms. At four acronyms the brain starts flailing like a spastic reindeer in an ice rink. You'll finish your entire conversation before your victim has decoded the first sentence.

You don't need to choose between ignorance and confusion. The two can be woven together to form a beautiful protective weasel tapestry. These powerful methods won't necessarily prove your innocence, but they might create *weasenable doubt,* and that's good enough.

Running Out the Clock

You might have noticed that tasks tend to "manage themselves" if given enough time. By that I mean that you can ignore almost everything that is asked of you and in the long run it won't matter. Either the tasks will become moot or your boss will forget what he asked you to do, or someone else will do it. This method of proactive ignoring, sometimes called ignorage, works even better if you are within two years of retirement, when you can run out the clock. In large companies you can postpone almost any task for two years without attracting suspicion. (Hey, things come up.) Remind people that you are "setting priorities" and there's nothing wrong with that. If you walk out of the company on your last day leaving a pile of unfinished work that is higher than your own leaping height, you win.

Depending on how long you need to stall, you want to select the weasel excuse that matches your time frame. Use this handy guide.

Stalling Guide

Excuse	Time It Buys You
Reorganization	One year
Lost the paperwork	One month
Illness	One week
In meetings	One day

These flexible excuses are suitable for all occasions. The typical weasel employee spends every day in meetings, coming down with ambiguous maladies, fretting about reorganizations, and discarding paperwork that looks important. It doesn't leave time for much else.

The best strategy is to use each of the excuses, starting with the lengthiest ones first. By the time you cycle through the list, another reorganization will be on the horizon and you can repeat. If you stall long enough, every corporate initiative ends, even layoffs. That's right: you can even run out the clock on your own layoff like this.

From my e-mail:

Dear Mr. Adams,

At one high-tech company the employees have been notified they will be laid off when they finish projects the company deems critical.
    How long do you think those projects will last?

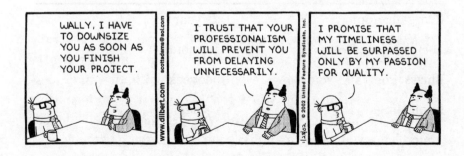

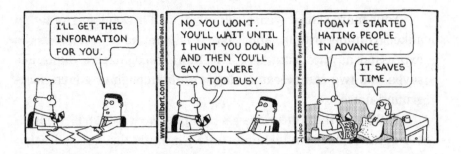

Incomprehensible Messages

From my e-mail:

> Dear Mr. Adams,
>
> I just got a voice mail from a person who spoke very fast at the beginning of his message, making his name unrecognizable, then the body of the message was normal, and then he sped up when giving his phone number, foiling me again.
>
> This is a great technique for appearing to be responsive while avoiding future contact.

When people want to hear back from you, they generally spell their name twice and repeat their phone number two or three times and sometimes even follow up with an e-mail message just to be sure. But when people never want to hear your voice again as long as they live, you get the alien-auctioneer mumble on your voice mail that sounds something like this:

"My number is *hsitfrninitayfreeohfreayh* . . . good-bye."

Your more skilled weasels know how to make all digits sound alike. Numbers four and five, for example, can both be expressed as the grunt *fuh*. The more recognizable digits like seven and two can be camouflaged with a cough or a loud background noise.

Failing in that, the weasel will sometimes transpose a number of his or her own telephone number. Later you'll assume that the weasel knows his own number so the problem must be on your end. Obviously you wrote it down wrong.

When weasels either don't know the answer to your question or don't want to research it, they will sometimes leave you incomprehensible scribbles on little yellow notes and then run away never to be seen again. It doesn't matter how simple and clear your question was—the answer can be made into an enigma. For example, you might leave a voice mail message asking for the cost of some item and get a handwritten note on your desk that looks like *Whq muth yagga epthyllp!* The exclamation mark is used to show that the weasel was enthusiastic about helping.

When leaving handwritten phone messages, the weasel will be careful to make sevens and ones look alike. Some weasels who want to cut down on incoming calls will go so far as to request personalized phone numbers like 555-1717.

Getting Back to You

A great weasel method for making people go away forever is saying, "I'll find that information and get back to you." Don't make the mistake of writing a note to yourself; that will ruin your later alibi of "I forgot." In fact, it's best if you make the promise while looking distracted. You want to send the clear impression that nothing being said is taking permanent hold in any part of your brain. Create the impression that the thought is going in one ear, turning into a false memory, then falling through a trapdoor into your esophagus and being harmlessly digested over about sixteen hours.

Returning Phone Calls

When you work for a big company, the only way to succeed is by begging dozens of people to do the one thing they hate above all else, i.e., their jobs. This system of begging for help and being ignored is called matrix management, or more colloquially, *"Answer the %@!*& phone, you lazy bastard!"* As a practical matter, matrix management involves hunting down coworkers who don't answer their phone and don't return calls until after your project is canceled.

People have learned to avoid answering the phone in matrix management situations because it's always someone asking them to do work. Incoming phone calls rarely involve people volunteering to help you. Nothing good can come from answering the phone.

If you were honest and left an outgoing voice mail message saying, "I'm selfish and busy. I will not return your message," then you would be fired. And if you returned all your calls promptly and allowed yourself to be sucked into helping other people succeed, your own projects would fail and you would be fired. This is a classic example where the Way of the Weasel is the only viable alternative.

Luckily for you there's no penalty for ignoring phone messages for months. Then, if you run into the ignoree in the elevator, you can say you were "just getting ready to call" or that he was "next on the list." Your only objective is to inject enough weasonable doubt into the situation that the ignoree can't expect a jury to side with him if he impales you with his umbrella.

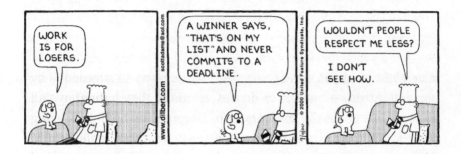

Coffee Weasels

If you have a coffee room in your office, you'll recognize this situation.

Dear Mr. Adams,

Here's the scenario. I'm already late for an important meeting. I run into the coffee room to get a cup of coffee and discover two pots, each with about a fourth of a cup of ever-thickening ooze. So I have to choose either to go to my meeting undercaffeinated or make a pot of coffee, wait for it to brew, and go to my meeting late. This choice came to me courtesy of the weasel that grabbed the last cup of drinkable coffee and slithered away without making a fresh pot.

Taking the last cup of coffee is one of the most difficult weasel maneuvers to pull off. The hard part is getting out of the coffee room undetected. Ideally, your office will have uncarpeted floors so you can hear footsteps approaching. Listen for a few seconds, and if it's quiet, you can safely make a clean getaway.

But if your work area is carpeted, and people can sneak up on you, it's good to have a backup weasel maneuver. Arrange the furniture in the coffee room so the garbage can is near the exit. Take the spent coffee grounds along with your ill-gotten last cup of drinkable coffee to the doorway and peer out. If no one is coming, drop the coffee grounds in the garbage (optionally, throw them against the wall just to see the splatter) and scamper away. But if anyone is approaching, wait until the he enters the doorway and then make a big deal about tossing away the grounds while announcing that you are "making a new pot of coffee, *again.*" You might even mention how much you hate the people who take the last cup and don't make a new pot. Then act as though your pager just vibrated, look at the incoming number with wide-eyed horror, and run out of the room mumbling, "Oh my God, oh my God."

The Kid Excuse

People who have children have the best work-avoidance excuses in the world. If you don't have kids, get some immediately. The playgrounds are full of them. They come with some baggage of their own, but there is no better excuse for missing work.

Kid-related excuses are so numerous and so flexible that you can concoct one on the spot anytime you need it, and it won't even necessarily be a lie. Kids always need one thing or another. For example, you could say, "My kid isn't feeling well." That's almost always true because kids are constantly hungry or sleepy or tired of making sneakers for sixteen hours a day. It's always something.

Anti-teamwork

All work begins as "potential work," and it's best to stomp it out as soon as you see it coming. Once it becomes "actual work," it's much harder to kill it. Most "potential work" will die from neglect if you just ignore it long enough. But the more virulent strains of potential work have to be handled with extreme prejudice.

You can smother potential work by skillfully applying a type of information called misinformation. Misinformation is exactly like regular information, except wrong.

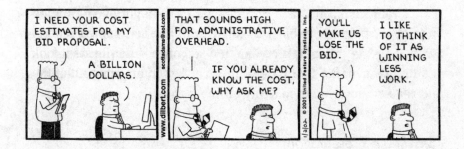

Don't get exotic in your misinformation. Stick with the basics of:

1. Costs too much

2. Lawsuits

3. Safety hazard

4. Physically impossible

Never say it will "be too much work" or "takes too long" because those sound exactly like "No problem" to everyone who doesn't need to do the work. And don't say, "There's no market demand," because there's some theoretical level of abuse that can make your salespeople sell anything.

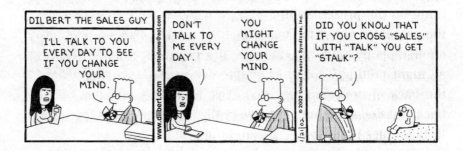

If your victim needs a better—i.e., more favorable—estimate from you, hold his project hostage until you get something you want, e.g., a budget increase for a coffee-fetching assistant, adding your name to a patent, or a roof on your cubicle. There's no reason you should go away empty-handed.

Stealing a Presentation

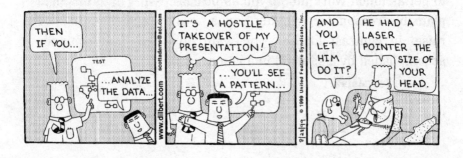

It's hard to create a wonderful business presentation. But it's easy to weasel in on one that's in progress and act as though you had something to do with creating it. The key to staging an unfriendly presentation takeover is to find a presenter, preferably a team member, who is too timid to confront you in front of a group of people. Use the excuse of wanting to point out something on the presentation and then walk to the front and scoot the presenter out of the way. Speak about the presentation with enough phony authority that it seems as though you had worked all night putting it together. Point your pen at someone toward the back of the room and say, "Yes, is there a question in the back?" It doesn't matter if there really is a question in the back. If that doesn't prompt an actual question, then say, "Oh. I thought you had a puzzled look on your face." That has the added weasel advantage of making the person you single out wonder for the rest of the day what is wrong with his or her face. And that's entertaining.

Objectives

If weasels had a dance, it would look exactly like you and your boss having a discussion about your objectives. Your boss wants to get as much work out of you as possible while maintaining a plausible reason for denying you a healthy and life-affirming raise. In contrast to that, you want objectives that could be accomplished by a squirrel in a coma.

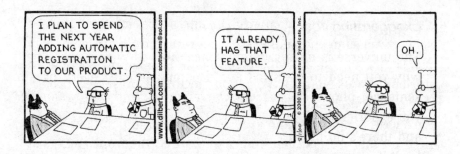

You'll never be held accountable for things that you can control, such as your effort and your dedication to the job. You *will* be accountable for the outcome of your efforts. And outcomes depend mostly on the screwups of others. For example, if your job involves working with a vendor, you hope you don't get an experienced salesperson who knows how to take your money and give you nothing in return. You want a salesperson who is so incompetent that you end up getting a good deal while the salesperson ends up getting fired by his boss.

It's also a big help if your coworkers are incompetent at whatever they're working on, as long as they aren't helping you. Their incompetence will allow you to get a bigger share of the budget. You'll need that to compensate for your boss's incompetence in getting enough funding for all the projects in the department.

And most of all, at the end of your project you'll need customers who are too dumb to know what they're buying. Realistically, any new product or process is hideously flawed. So in the beginning you need customers who—against all reason—don't seem to mind paying for defective products.

Exaggerating Your Accomplishments

The universe is mostly empty space, and so is your job. That's why you need to claim as an "accomplishment" every breath, sentence, phone call, casual conversation, and bodily function you experience. No one loves you as much as you love yourself, and there's no penalty for bragging. You might even get a raise for it if you word it right.

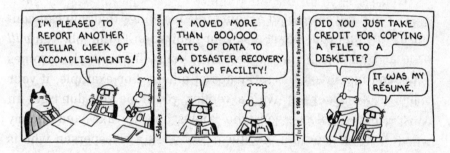

Sick Days

Show me a company that offers paid time off for sickness and I'll show you a company that's bristling with sick weasels.

Sick days: Vacation days for weasels.

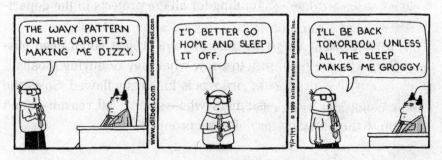

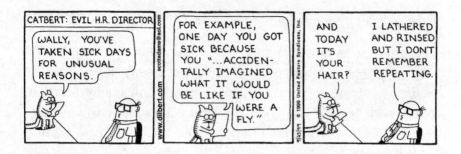

Weasels have an uncanny ability to get sick for exactly the number of days their companies allow as sick days per year. "Sick" is a highly subjective concept. If you're a normal human, there's almost always something wrong with you. And like a fine wine, sick day excuses get better with age. Toward the end of your career your boss will be surprised if you ever make it to work without some part of your body falling off. Age makes a whole host of new illnesses available to you—everything from pacemakers to hip replacements, even if you don't need them. Medical insurance covers hospital expenses, and you'll be unconscious during the unpleasant parts, so why not be proactive? There's no reason to stop replacing your body parts with machine parts until you're technically considered a cyborg, at which point you lose voting rights.

One mistake that rookie weasels make is to use the same sickness excuse too many times. It's easy to forget what excuse you already used. I recommend taking your fake illnesses in alphabetical order so you don't inadvertently repeat:

Appendicitis . . . Bronchitis . . . Cholera . . .
Diphtheria . . . etc.

Dear Mr. Adams,

I have a coworker who takes advantage of the system at every chance. She has been known to take off sick because she had "puffy" lips.

The trick to sounding sick on the phone is to leave a voice mail for your boss within thirty seconds of waking up. If you're like me, you routinely have the following symptoms each and every time you wake up in the morning:

1. Aching muscles

2. Pounding headache

3. No energy

4. Funky voice

5. Depression

After two sips of coffee I'm feeling fine. But that first thirty seconds is indistinguishable from the last moment before dying of black plague. If you make the call during that period, your boss will actually thank you for staying home.

The main risk in taking sick days is that whatever weasel schemes you have cooking at work might require your presence to keep them bubbling along. Like this:

Dear Mr. Adams,

I worked with a fellow I shall call Weaselbert whose cube was the model of efficiency and neatness. Our Pointy-Haired Boss (PHB) often pointed out to the rest of us how Weaselbert had organized all of his work into carefully marked loose-leaf binders. Each binder was the same size and color and each was labeled on the spine with its contents.

   We kept telling our PHB that this guy was a weasel, but the PHB thought he was GREAT, and every couple weeks, the PHB would make a point of commenting about Weaselbert's wonderfully organized cube. Oh, how the PHB wished we were all as organized as Weaselbert. PHB would even take visitors in to see how organized the cube was.

   So . . . here's the good part. One day Weaselbert was on vacation and the PHB asked for some information that I didn't have. I told him I did not know where to get the report he wanted. He got really pissed and practically dragged me over to Weaselbert's cube to show me the binder where I could get the report he wanted. When the PHB pulled the binder out of the bookcase, it was EMPTY. Every binder was EMPTY. PHB then opened up the file cabinet. The files were all carefully marked and were all EMPTY. In the bottom drawer of the weasel's desk was a huge pile of paper with all of his work in one disgusting dog-eared, coffee-stained stack. I thought the PHB was going to have a stroke!

   Needless to say all of the weasel's coworkers were in the office at oh-dark-thirty the next Monday morning to make sure we were there when Weaselbert got back from vacation. No one wanted to miss the fireworks.

Avoiding Teamwork

Whether in your professional or personal life, there will always be weasels trying to get you to do some of their work under the guise of "teamwork." The best weasel method for avoiding teamwork is to cheerfully accept any request for help and then start asking "questions" about the direction of the task. Make it clear that you think you're there to help not just with the little stuff but—because you're a great team player—also with the global strategy implications.

This method works just as well at home. For example, if your spouse asks you to help move a couch to the other side of the room, happily accept the job. Then start questioning the wisdom of owning a couch at all. Rub your chin and look at the fabric of the couch and suggest that it's time to have it reupholstered. And it wouldn't be a bad idea to get it Scotchgarded and maybe someone should vacuum under the cushions. Try to achieve a ratio of ten minutes of debating for every one minute of actual helping.

In time your spouse or coworker will learn that asking you to help is an invitation to psychological torture. And all the while you will be viewed as "helpful."

Best of all, when people complain about "the way you are," it will come off as sounding petty. It's difficult to generate a plausible complaint about someone who is too helpful.

Gradually Shifting

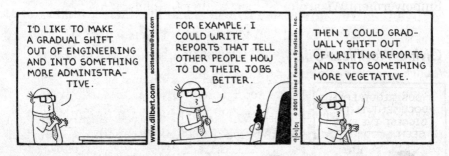

Weasels often try to "gradually shift" from whatever job they don't like into work that is more pleasant. Weasels who are gradually shifting to other jobs are difficult to fire because they are doing work—just not the work for which they were hired.

The key to the gradual shift strategy is not asking permission. The weasel simply does a little less of the job for which he's paid and a little bit more of the job that's more pleasant, ideally a new job that exists only in the weasel's mind. That way the weasel isn't stepping on any toes. And because it's gradual, his boss has lots of time to get used to it. It sneaks up on everyone. Finally, one day the weasel proclaims that he no longer does the old job.

This strategy depends on having a boss who doesn't like confrontation. The weasel must control his rate of gradual shift so that it is just slightly below the level that would make a busy boss want to think about it.

The end goal of the gradual shift weasel tactic is to get paid for something that requires no business travel and no writing things down. The gradual shift weasel wants the sort of job that involves getting invited to meetings and giving opinions. This usually involves inventing some sort of unique job title, like Empowerment Wizard or Subject Matter Ombudsman.

Giving Worthless Gifts

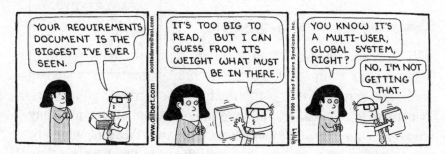

I recently read a book called *Age of Propaganda*. One of the techniques for persuasion involves giving people things they didn't ask for, thus triggering a psychological need to reciprocate; then you sell them something they don't want. Amazingly, that trick actually works. People are so conditioned to giving something in return for receiving something that they have trouble controlling the impulse.

You can use that trick at work. The best sort of thing to give is something of no financial value whatsoever, such as magazine clippings. A well-chosen magazine clipping gives the impression that you put thought into the "gift" even though you spent no money whatsoever. If someone starts leaving you lots of clippings, you're probably going to be asked for something. That's why I always keep a few clippings with me in my wallet in case I'm ambushed by a clipping-giver. I just whip out a clipping of my own and reciprocate immediately.

I say, "Thanks for the clipping on how to make fuel out of methane gas. Here's a little clipping for you about the rising cost of cotton. Mine is longer than yours, but you can make it up to me later."

Evaluating a Vendor's Product

The first step in evaluating a vendor's product is to figure out who in your company is related to the vendor, who is sleeping with the vendor, who got bribed by the vendor, who is best friends with the vendor, and who hopes to someday work for the vendor. If any of those people are you, or someone in higher management, the evaluation is greatly simplified. You declare that it's one heckuva good product and buy it.

Most vendor comparisons involve an expensive alternative that has only a few problems versus a cheaper alternative with lots of problems. So there's always something to love about every choice. Therefore a skilled weasel can get approval for anything by emphasizing the positive. The important thing is to avoid wasting time trying to get approval for a doomed choice. Here's a cautionary tale.

Dear Mr. Adams,

Upper management told us to try to use a particular vendor's software in our environment. We knew from prior meetings and discussions that the proposed new software wouldn't work—whereas another software would work fine—but we went about the evaluation anyway. After spending countless hours and piles of money trying to do what we were told, we discovered what we already knew— that we couldn't use the suggested vendor's software in our environment.

Later we found out that our boss's boss's boss's spouse is on the directors' board of that software distribution company.

Back Pay for Weasels

When I say *"back* pay," I mean getting paid disability insurance for claiming you hurt your back on the job. Back injuries are the perfect weasel scheme because they're hard to disprove. Scientists don't even understand how backs work. To the untrained eye a back looks simple, like a bunch of muscles with some doughnut-shaped bones over a long rod of spinal gook. But in fact, the human back is more of a mystery than why there's a tiny punching bag hanging in the back of your throat.

The best time to fake a back injury is a week before you know you're going to get fired for incompetence (assuming there is no severance package). From that moment on, you're a protected species, like the red squirrels eating my roof, only more rodent-like. Your employer will be afraid to fire you after you've been injured on the job because it will look like retaliation for making your disability insurance go up. It's the perfect weasel trap.

The insurance company might skulk around your house with a video camera trying to catch you being active. So it's a good idea to keep up appearances. For example, when you're golfing, after every putt, grab your back and throw yourself on the green and writhe in agony. The other people in your foursome will just think you're a poor sport when in fact you are an ultraclever weasel who is being paid to not work.

Getting Fired for a Living

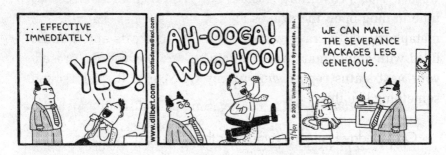

If your company is in a death spiral and looking to get rid of employees, it might beef up the severance package until you find it irresistible. That's when you need to *stop* sabotaging the careers of your coworkers and *start* sabotaging yourself so you can get fired and get that money.

Start with small changes such as making your appearance less professional. If you're a woman, tuck your blouse into the back of your panty hose and glue a four-foot length of toilet paper to the bottom of your shoe. Vary the length of the toilet paper every day so it looks like a recurring problem. Extend your lipstick beyond your lip line until someone asks if you're plotting to kill Batman. For a hairstyle I recommend something in the "matted" family with just a hint of infestation.

If you're a man—and your boss is a woman—wear unappealing shoes to work. Women don't like to be around men with substandard footwear. Women won't admit this, but they consider the men around them to be free-range accessories for their own outfits. If you clash, you're hash.

If your ratty appearance doesn't move you to the front of the canning line, then it's time to take drastic action: stop being a weasel. That's right; forget about hiding your incompetence. It's time to fling open the drapes and show your boss that you are, metaphorically, a crazy woman with fifty-four cats and a house filled with empty margarine containers. In other words, present your next status report *without* any weaseleze. It might sound something like this:

> On Monday I couldn't remember the lyrics to a song that was in my head so I spent the day researching it on the Web until eventually I forgot the melody too. On Tuesday people kept calling me and leaving messages, but when I called them back, they weren't there. Wednesday I had a doctor's appointment to find out why I'm gaining weight. The doctor thinks it's related to my massive consumption of food. I have more tests scheduled for next week. I spent all day Thursday in a meeting that turned out to be the wrong meeting. I realized my mistake after the fourth hour, but by then I was passionately committed to their Mission Statement so I stayed. And that brings us to today, where I have spent most of the day typing this status report.

Your employer might try to counter your weasel plan with a weasel move of his own, like this:

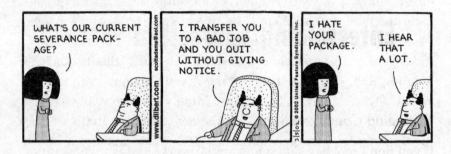

2

Entertaining Yourself at Work

Criticizing Coworkers

If you don't feel like doing any actual work, and yet you want to appear "useful," you can spend your workday criticizing coworkers, i.e., weasel work. It's both easy and entertaining and it shows your dedication to teamwork.

Luckily for you, your coworkers are no better at their jobs than you are at yours. So there's plenty of material to work with.

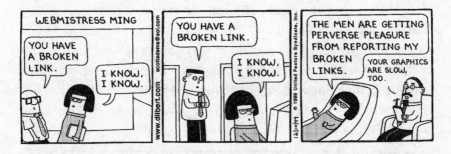

Try to resist the urge to laugh out loud as you enjoy your God-given right of making other people feel like losers. Pick out some obvious problems with a coworker's performance and then suggest the most unpleasant solution imaginable. For example:

"Gee, Carl, it looks like your customers and vendors aren't on the same page. You should host a conference somewhere in the middle of their locations, like Iraq, to work out all of the differences."

Later, when your coworker runs into problems with his project, you can remind him that you suggested a solution but it was "ignored." Then shake your head in disgust and shuffle away.

Taking Training

If you get a kick out of making your boss nervous, take training classes. Bosses know that when you display an appetite for learning, it means one thing: you're planning to leave for a better job.

Your pointy-haired boss would prefer that you remain slightly incompetent because incompetence is less expensive than training, and incompetent employees can't leave for better jobs. And when your boss wants to experience the joy of criticizing subordinates, untrained employees are a target-rich environment.

That's why you should sign up for training classes at every opportunity, such as when your boss is on vacation. Training is easier than working—especially if you don't pay attention to the instructor—and it makes your boss squirm. That's a win-win scenario. After the training, drop hints of your impending departure such as "Those training classes have made me see how wonderful the world is—*out there.*"

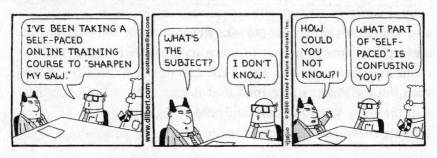

Attractiveness

Attractive people have special weasel privileges because the rest of us like to look at them. No one wants to take a chance of angering good-looking people because if they go someplace else, then we'll have to sit around looking at each other. And that's not entertaining.

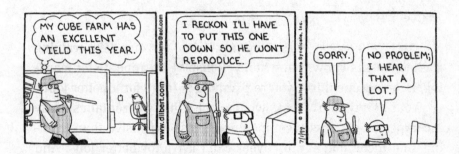

Have you ever noticed that attractive people leave early from any gathering? If it's a long meeting, they leave during the first break. If it's a party, they leave halfway through. Sometimes they say they're planning to attend but they don't show up.

I first noticed this effect when I was in my early twenties. At that age I didn't dare talk during meetings because I didn't know what any of the buzzwords meant. I could sit in a meeting for three hours and leave without even knowing what the topic had been. I compensated for my complete worthlessness by nodding and sometimes pretending to take notes. For me, the only way to survive the boredom was to stare at attractive women in the room and fantasize that they lusted after short, confused men with thick glasses. I imagined that if they only got to know the real me, they would understand that I have no discernible personality either, and it would be a turn-on.

   Unfortunately my survival method only worked for the first half of every meeting. After the break, the attractive women were always gone. I survived by fashioning a tiny simulated supermodel using a pencil and two plastic dairy-creamer containers. But it wasn't the same.

Agreeing

If you spend all of your time arguing with people who are nuts, you'll be exhausted and the nuts will still be nuts. That's why you should learn to agree with people who are nuts, e.g., your boss. But you don't need to agree in a humiliating suck-up way. You can agree in a way that entertains you, like this:

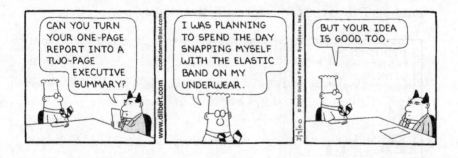

3

Getting Your Way at Work

Business Analysis

Someday you might be forced to do a business analysis in order to get what you want. The word *analysis* is formed by the root word *anal* and the ancient Greek work *ysis*, meaning "to pull numbers from." That's a good description of every business analysis I've ever seen, especially the ones I wrote.

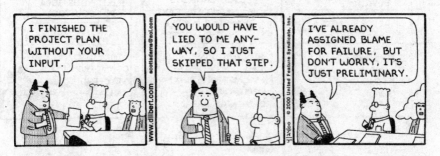

But just because all numbers are yanked directly from someone's colon, that doesn't mean the resulting conclusions are wrong. Managers have an effective system of checks and balances so that bad numbers can be corrected by using faulty assumptions and poor logic. If that isn't enough, heavy doses of rounding and spreadsheet formula errors will usually close the gap.

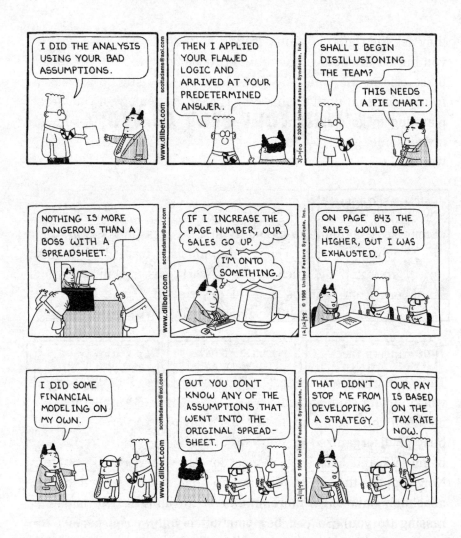

Before you can deceive the public with your business analysis, you might need to deceive your own senior executives. Your best strategy is to divert their attention away from the areas where you made up the numbers and hope they get bored before they ask the right questions. If they start sniffing too near where you buried the bodies, mention a problem you've noticed someplace else in the company and see if you can stir up a weasel frenzy over that until the meeting is over. By analogy, if you were planning to go sailing in shark-infested waters, you'd want to invite some guests who are slow swimmers and have open wounds.

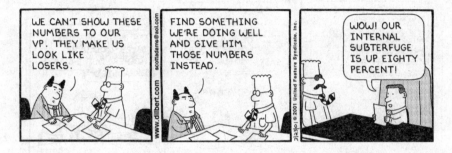

Time

Time is the weasel's favorite tool. For example, let's say you're working with someone who prefers arriving late for all appointments. If you asked him, he'd say it's not a preference—he's just busy or disorganized or unlucky. That's weaselspeak for "I like being late and I have no respect for any other living human." Now suppose the two of you have an important meeting and you absolutely have to get there on time or it will be horribly embarrassing (to you). So you beg your often-late weasel partner to promise that just this once he will be on time. What will happen?

He will promise. Then *something will come up.*

The late weasel will swear that he left for the meeting with time to spare but he got a flat tire, was hit by a meteor, or realized halfway to the meeting that he wasn't wearing pants. The weird thing is that the excuses generally check out. You can go to the weasel's house and examine his wrecked car and see the meteor still embedded in the engine block. Individually the excuses of weasels are completely understandable. It's only collectively that you notice that meteors only hit people who prefer being late.

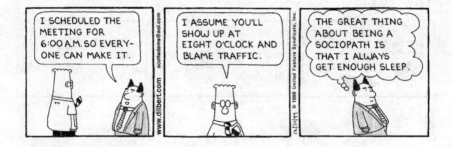

Business Politeness

The biggest problem in the business world is that there are no socially accepted ways to tell coworkers to leave your cubicle. The workplace would be nearly nirvana if that flaw was corrected. I'm an advocate of inventing new social conventions whenever you need them, not waiting around for centuries until one day you realize they exist. I propose the following social standards for immediate adoption by the entire business world.

For Getting People out of Your Cube. After someone has overstayed his welcome in your cubicle, raise one hand in the "stop" position, then roll the wrist and give a dismissive back-of-hand motion coupled with an audible "Bah!" Let's all agree that this is the polite way of saying, in effect, "Although your constant babbling about yourself and your problems is fascinating, I think you should be someplace else, possibly writing it all down into a script for a miniseries so the whole world can share the joy I am now experiencing."

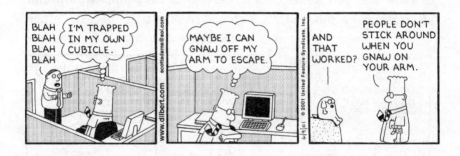

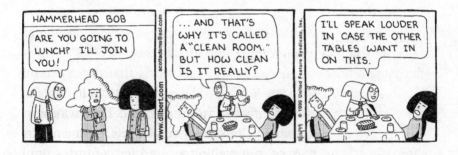

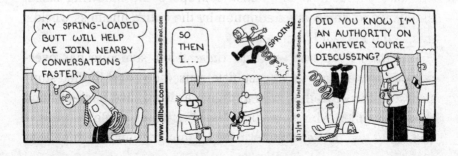

For Telling People They Are Full of $#!!* When a lying weasel is shoveling huge wheelbarrows of nonsense at you, turn your back and use one foot to mime that you are kicking sand in his direction, like a cat covering his work in a sandbox. We should all agree that this means, "Your version of reality is creative and stimulating. I am sure that if someday scientists discover other universes, then what you say will be proven true. I for one am willing to wait until that day."

Customer Tour

Most activities have an obvious purpose. A blazing exception to that rule is the "customer tour" of an office. It's not clear why weasels insist that you look at their office space. If a weasel has an office that is somehow remarkable, it *might* be worth a look, for about thirty seconds. But weasels generally insist on giving one-hour guided museum tours that go like this.

> **Weasel:**   On your left we have a bunch of cubicles. On your right we have a bunch of cubicles. Behind them you can see a wall. I have a funny story about the ductwork . . .

Your best defense is to threaten to never buy another product unless the tour ends immediately.

I can't figure out what the tour-givers are up to. Maybe weasels are trying to stretch ten minutes of agenda into two hours so the customer won't get mad about having traveled a thousand miles. Maybe weasels hate customers. I don't know. I will study this matter and get back to you.

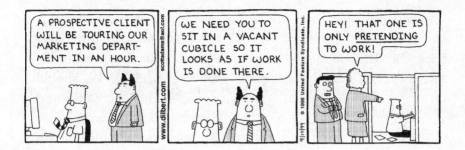

Weasel Suggestions

For every person who thinks up a magnificent breakthrough idea, there are a hundred people who are nothing more than mindless and unimportant implementers of the idea. The reason for the imbalance in numbers is that the implementers tend to kill the people with the great ideas in order to cut down on the workload.

Dear Mr. Adams,

For several years, I submitted plans and suggestions to my boss to enable electronic access to procurement contracts. Not seeing any opportunity for self-aggrandizement, my Pointy-Haired Boss never promoted the plan. One day a weasel coworker took my plan to another department whose boss approved it. They both received $2,500 suggestion awards, and the plan was sent to me for implementation.

Ambiguity

If you forget to tell someone about an important deadline until it's too late, and it's clearly your fault, try this trick for introducing some weasonable doubt about your guilt. Apologize for "not reminding" your victim of the deadline, meeting, or task. This sounds like an apology while sending the following message:

1. I already told you once.

2. You (the victim) probably forgot I told you.

3. You (the victim) are such an idiot that I ought to realize I need to tell you things over and over again.

If your victim protests your choice of words and says that you never mentioned the deadline, contort your face into a sympathetic expression that signals, "You poor forgetful soul. I pity you."

And once again take full responsibility, in a weasel way, by saying, "I often forget things like that." That still leaves open the possibility that while you forget things *like* that you did not forget *that*.

Inoculating Your Boss

Unless a person *is* your boss the only leverage that person has over you is the threat of complaining *to* your boss. This threat is especially effective if your boss already knows that you're a stinkin' weasel and likely to be guilty of any charge against you.

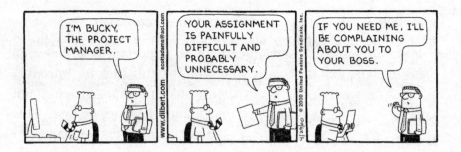

As soon as you start working with someone who you suspect might later complain about you, inoculate your boss with stories of how your evil coworker has a habit of fabricating lies. Mention that you saw some medication in his wastebasket, apparently unused. All you know is that "it sure wasn't aspirin."

Anytime this potential rat says anything in the vicinity of your boss, make the "he's nuts" gesture by swirling your finger next to your head. It doesn't matter what your coworker is saying when you do it because most things sound nuts if you stop to think about them.

Abusing People's Optimism

About once a week I get a call from someone that I work with who says something like, "*Time* magazine called. They want to do an interview with you and put your face on the cover!" This gets me all excited and I call my parents to tell them to look for my face on the cover of *Time* magazine. I say something like, "They didn't come right out and say I'm Man of the Year, Mom, but I think that's implied."

When I call the reporter, it soon becomes clear that this wasn't *Time* magazine; it was actually for the *Time* magazine Web site. But still, that's pretty good, so I agree to the interview.

Later, while doing the interview, I learn that the reporter doesn't actually work for the *Time* magazine Web site. He's a freelancer who hopes to sell his story to them. He's never sold a story to anyone before, but he feels lucky this time.

Weaselmath

If you were the proprietor of the Pocket Lint Museum in California, and you wanted to tout your popularity, you wouldn't say, "Visited by over three people per year and they only stopped to ask directions!" You would replace the small number three with the much larger number 12 million, as in "Located in a state with over 12 million tourists per year!" The beauty of weaselmath is that relevancy isn't important.

Weaselmath: Replacing small numbers with large numbers.

Here's a recent example from real life. I'm co-owner of a restaurant in Pleasanton, California—Stacey's Café. One day a salesman for a local radio station was trying to convince my managing partner and me to buy advertising. I asked how many listeners they have. I figured that was a normal question to ask in that situation. How do you think the salesman responded? Did he . . .

1. Give me a useful range of listener numbers so I could judge the value of my advertising investment

or

2. Act as if no one had ever asked that question and argue that it wasn't important?

The sales weasel went for option two. Then, with mild condescension he explained, "You have to spend money to make money."

I pointed out that he probably knew the number of listeners and that I could decide on my own if it was worth knowing. The weasel responded by explaining how many human beings lived within listening range of his station, i.e., weaselmath. I asked how that mattered if they weren't *actually* listening, just *potentially* listening.

Then he explained that it's much more expensive to advertise on other radio stations on a cost-per-relevant-listener basis. I asked how he knew that if he didn't know how many listeners he had.

He explained to me that some of my competitors were advertising on his station and they must be getting some benefit or they wouldn't be doing it. I pointed out that most of my competitors *weren't* advertising on his station and if *not advertising* wasn't working, they wouldn't be doing it.

It wasn't what you would call a "good meeting."

Within a week of writing the section above, another perfect example of weaselmath came my way. I was booked to appear on a national morning talk show. Unfortunately, because of time zone differences, I would have to wake up at around 2:30 A.M. to make it to the location on time. One of my business associates, wanting me to feel motivated for this sacrifice, reminded me by e-mail that it's worthwhile because "10 million people would be watching." Being the incredulous weasel-sniffer that I am, I questioned that number, knowing that any number that is evenly divisible by ten is completely made up. This turned out to be the case, but upon checking with the producers of the show my associate assured me the "viewership is between 4 and 5 million."

Let me interpret that from weaseltalk to English: *During the course of the entire program, 4.01 million people (that's between 4 and 5 million) will see at least one minute of the show ON A GOOD DAY.* So the total number of people who would see my promised three-minute segment (which ended up being one and a half minutes) is probably one-tenth of the original motivating estimate of 10 million. And it illustrates an important point. Most weaselmath is at least ten times larger than the actual number.

In a similar vein, a producer for a fledgling cable TV show recently asked me to appear on one of its shows. I asked how large their audience is and she said the network was "available" to 25 million people.

Exercise:
Convert the weaselmath estimate of "available to 25 million viewers" to the nonweasel actual viewership number. Which answer is closest?

A. Nobody

B. Just your immediate family

C. Nobody

Data

The most worthless kind of data is the accurate kind. The whole point of collecting data is to persuade people to do something they're not already doing. Accurate data won't change anyone's mind about anything, especially if you make the mistake of putting it in context. Luckily there are solutions to accurate data.

From my e-mail:

Dear Mr. Adams,

I worked for a company that was responsible for maintaining and supplying data extracts from a database for a telecommunications company. A colleague of mine found a bug in one of the data extract programs. He spent days tracking it down and confirmed that he'd fixed it by reconciling figures produced by the rogue extract with data from other sources. Was the customer grateful? No, they weren't, because the new figures "were not what they were expecting." My colleague had to put the bug back in and re-extract the data to replace the data from the fixed extract.

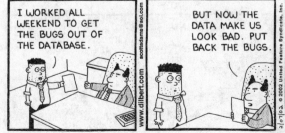 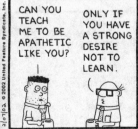

If you don't want to spend money to intentionally pollute your good data until it becomes useful, don't worry. A skilled professional can abuse good data until it is almost as useful as bad data. For example, let's say a bookstore decides to order this book and doesn't know how wildly popular it will be. The buyer could hedge his risk by ordering a small number—say three copies—and later ordering more if needed. At the end of the month the publisher's sales agent will visit the bookstore.

> **Sales Agent:**   You sold one hundred percent of your supply. You should order huge truckloads of additional copies so you don't keep running out.
>
> **Bookstore**   Are you nuts? We only sold *three* copies of
> **Buyer:**   this book in a whole month!

Both weasels are using the same accurate data, and yet neither one has any idea what is the right number of books to reorder, so it's a stalemate. That's when the sales agent needs to resort to weaselmath.

> **Sales Agent:**   My God, don't you realize there are four billion people on earth who know how to read? I recommend buying the eight-pack.

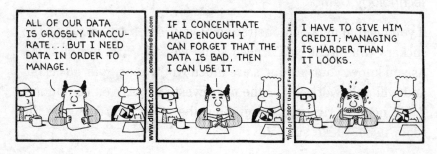

The Weasel Creep Method

The weasel creep method involves promising to change—to do something less annoying, more helpful, or less illegal, and then, over time, gradually going back to doing whatever you were doing in the first place.

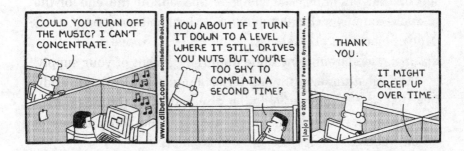

The weasel creep method works best for things that are difficult to quantify, such as noisiness, neatness, rudeness, and laziness. On any given day you can claim with a straight face that you are being no more of a weasel than the day before. Moreover, your accuser is "suddenly springing this" on you. And there's nothing fair about that.

Technology Demo

If you need to do a demonstration of your company's products so suckers will buy it, you'll need some weasel tricks to pull it off. As you know, your products are much worse than your ads claim and will only work under the narrowest of contrived conditions. You'll need to rig everything about the demo, starting with the room itself. Make sure the temperature, windchill factor, lighting, ambient noise, and floor vibrations are carefully controlled. The slightest imperfection in any of those factors could cause your product to break into shards and impale potential buyers. As a general rule, when people are impaled by a product, it makes them less likely to become repeat customers.

Secondly, keep your product away from the filthy and unpredictable fingers of anyone who is not thoroughly trained in what to avoid touching. One tap of a wrong button could create a cascade of electrical problems that will erase hard disks, set off fire alarms, and summon the undead.

And most importantly, try to smile and have fun. Ignore the fact that any number of looming disasters with the demo could ruin your company, your career, and your last hope for propagating your genes.

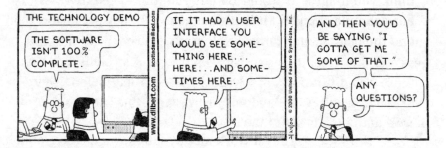

Weaselstistics

I saw a clever bit of pro-gun* humor bouncing around the Internet without attribution. The gist of the e-mail is that the number

---

*Because I know you're wondering, I'm in favor of gun ownership for everyone including felons. But I believe only cartoonists should have ammo.

of accidental deaths per physician is nine thousand times higher than the number of accidental deaths per gun owner, so doctors should be banned.

For those of you who are satire-impaired—and believe me, you don't know who you are—I will translate: the author was making the point that you have to consider both the good *and* the bad when forming an opinion. Otherwise your friends will start wearing T-shirts that say "I'm with stupid" and you won't understand why.

Now, those of you who like guns are thinking the author of the pro-gun humor piece is a genius and a champion of freedom, and those of you who are antigun are thinking he's a future serial killer. If you can let go of those feelings for a minute and look at his point about considering both sides of any argument, I think you'll agree it would be entertaining to see more of that. For example, wouldn't it be fun to hear a CEO describe the good *and* the bad of some decision? It might sound like this.

> *CEO:* We've decided to close our last factory in this country and move production to a place where the locals have never heard of money. They'll work all day long for a chance to look at a shiny object. We plan to downsize thousands of loyal workers in this country, but I'm not worried because I live behind a huge gate.

Wouldn't that be refreshing?

Planting Ideas

No one wants to use someone else's idea. That means doing a bunch of work and then having someone else claim credit for "thinking of it." So if you want your idea to be used, you have to trick other people into thinking they thought of it first. Luckily this is easy.

You start by suggesting a fragment of an idea that is missing something obvious or has a clear flaw. Then you let the other person fix the idea, thus making it his own. Then praise "his idea" to seal the deal.

Example: Let's say you want your off-site business meeting to be held at the seaside town of Monterey but you know that if you suggest it, your boss will reject it because it came from you.

> **You:** Maybe we should hold the meeting near a body of water, such as a puddle or a glass of water.
>
> **Boss:** No, too small. How about an ocean?
>
> **You:** Yes!! An ocean could work. And it could be in Utah.
>
> **Boss:** Utah? That's too far. How about California?
>
> **You:** Yes!! No wonder you're the boss. Maybe it could be in that town . . . what's it called . . . Montezuma or Mantoya?
>
> **Boss:** Forget those places. Let's go to Monterey!
>
> **You:** (grumbling) No one ever uses *my* ideas.

Signaling Your Lack of Importance

Sometimes it is necessary for a leader to inform workers of their relative lack of importance.

From my e-mail:

> Mr. Adams,
>
> My boss explained to me last night about how she deliberately delays responding to e-mails by varying amounts of time, just to impress upon people their relative standing in terms of power.

You can tell what rank you hold in the corporation by how people react to you when you enter their office and find them on the phone.

If He or She . . .	Then You Are . . .
Greets you immediately, apologizes to the caller, and ends phone call	Very important
Gives you the "just one minute" finger signal and finishes call in a leisurely fashion	Important
Asks for your pen and then throws it into the hallway, and after you retrieve it you discover the door has been closed and locked	Not important

Weasel Knowledge

If you take a bunch of ignorance and mix it with PowerPoint charts, you get weasel knowledge. Weasel knowledge is to actual knowledge what a painting of a diamond is to the actual diamond.

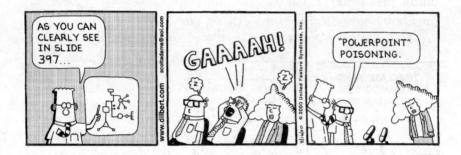

For every type of ignorance there is some theoretical amount of formatting that will make it look brilliant. The specific technique is beyond the scope of this book, but it involves fonts.

You can compensate for a lack of useful information by increasing the number of PowerPoint slides you use. After about a dozen slides your audience will slip into a trancelike state and fantasize about the afterlife. Anything you say after that will slither past their conscious minds and go directly into the subconscious, where it will burrow in, build a home, and years later show up on X rays as a tumor.

Weasel Faces

The best tool a weasel can have is a face that naturally says, "I'm not a weasel. Really, I'm not." People are born with faces that send all sorts of messages, from "I'm happy to be alive" to "I am harboring a hideous secret." My face, unfortunately, causes people to recoil in horror and shriek, "My God! What horrible thing have you done?!" That is a hindrance to my weasel ambitions and a large part of the reason I'm a cartoonist—so people don't see my face. I've spent hours of mirror time trying to look like I didn't just order a contract killing. The best I can get is an uncanny impression of Tom Petty on heroin.

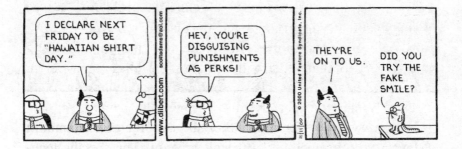

Defining the Issue

If you know you've done something horribly wrong, or you think you might do something wrong later, you'll want to use a weasel technique called defining the issue. It's used in politics all the time and it works just as well in the workplace. The method relies on the fact that people are so dim-witted they believe that whatever they hear about the most is also the most important thing. Your goal is to guide people into spending time thinking about something other than your shortcomings.

For example, let's say that you are always late because you have no respect for other people or you're just generally incompetent. You don't want tardiness to besmirch your reputation.

Instead, when you start a new job, you could set the stage by talking about how you're such a perfectionist. Keep mentioning how it's such a burden to always need to have everything right. Then, when your pattern of lateness emerges, you can define the issue as being a natural result of your need to "get everything exactly perfect." That's not nearly as bad as being an inconsiderate weasel, and if you talk about it often enough, it will seem like an obvious truth to your coworkers.

Or let's say you expect to be way over budget by the end of the year. You need to start early to define the problem as a lack of management support and not a colossal screwup on your part. At every opportunity you should tell your manager and your coworkers that you are underfunded because management is too blind to see "what this sort of thing costs if you want to do it right." When your performance review rolls around, you can argue that you are not a person who is over budget, you're a visionary who is much better than your boss at predicting budgets. An especially bold weasel might list this skill as an accomplishment and use it as justification to ask for a raise.

Either-Or Weasels

I just got an e-mail invitation from what I call an either-or weasel. She noticed I would be giving a speech in her local area and wanted to set up a meeting with me to discuss unspecified business about some sort of unspecified event at an unspecified time in the future. The only thing I knew for sure is that it would involve work.

As you know, lack of specificity is one of the weasel's greatest tricks. It's hard to say no to something until you know what it is.

That's why bad offers never have details. When facing an either-or weasel, most people would make the mistake of declining the vague invitation to meet and offering some sort of "reason" such as being busy. That won't work. It's a trap. The weasel would immediately respond to the reason of being too busy with an offer of flexibility. The weasel will meet *any*time, either before or after. It's hard to say you're too busy for a two-minute meeting with someone who's that accommodating. So you're trapped by your own "too busy" excuse.

The either-or approach is a time-honored weasel technique. It's most often used for selling things that people don't want. The weasel offers you two choices that both mean yes. For example, in my case the weasel offered to meet me either *before* or *after* my public appearance. That form of a question tricks the brain into considering which choice to pick instead of whether to meet at all.

Luckily I am an experienced weasel. I countered with another weasel trick that I call selective ignoring. I responded to her e-mail by asking what she wanted to discuss, ignoring the question of when to meet.

Now the weasel is on the other foot. If she accuses me of ignoring her question, she will appear pushy. That will work against her goal of persuading me to do something I don't want to do. And importantly, now she knows she's dealing with a skilled weasel. So she has to take it up a level.

She could counter my selective ignoring with some selective ignoring of her own and say, "I can explain what it's about when I see you. Is before or after your speech the best for you?"

Or she might mail me a gift so I feel the need to reciprocate. But I'm one step ahead and already plan not to receive her next message due to technical difficulties.

Being the Bank

Sometimes weasels can get free meals, merchandise, and even airline miles by volunteering to "be the bank" during business meals and celebrations. The way this works is you agree to collect money from everyone toward some collective expense and then pay the bill on your credit card. If you get airline miles for your charge amounts, that's your first weasel benefit. The rest works the way this victim describes it.

> Dear Mr. Adams,
>
> Several coworkers and I were traveling to a business meeting and we stopped for lunch. When it came time to pay the bill, each of us had cash to cover our meals except for one person. She said she'd take our cash and pay using her credit card. Those of us with cash had included our shares of the tip, so we practically covered the entire bill, excluding the tip. As we were leaving the restaurant, I glanced at the line on the receipt where she left the tip. She had left a measly $3.00. So essentially, my coworker not only screwed our server, but she also got a relatively expensive meal for only a few bucks.
>
> I'm SO glad I was able to subsidize her weaselly ways.

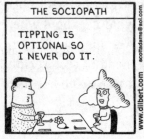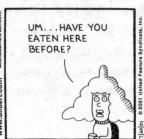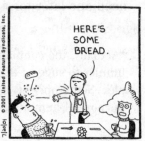

Conference Room Etiquette

When I worked at the phone company, I had a coworker who used conference rooms for preconjugal visits. He was my hero. His girlfriend worked for the company too, so technically he was using company resources for nonbusiness purposes.* And they both got paid for it. That's why your phone bill is so high. Watch now as I smoothly transition into my topic . . .

Conference rooms are like love, i.e., hard to find, and far more enjoyable if doughnuts are involved. In most companies there are too many people searching for too few conference rooms. One weasel solution is preemptive booking, like this:

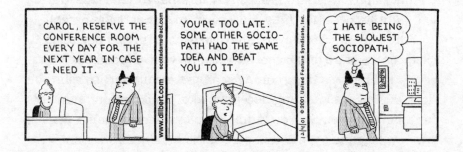

Your company probably has some sort of conference room reservation system. Weasels will game the system by inventing fake meeting titles and reserving the rooms just in case they need one later for a real meeting. Once all the conference rooms

---

*Actually, the company resources were using each other. But it sounds funnier to suggest that his girlfriend was in the same category as a stapler. Sometimes it is necessary to dehumanize people for the higher purpose of humor.

have been booked in perpetuity with fake meetings, and it's impossible to hold real meetings, you'll have a perfect excuse for ignoring the input of your coworkers. They'll probably complain that they "weren't consulted" about your decisions. They might even try to organize a meeting to decide what to do about you. But they won't be able to find a meeting room. *Buwhahaha!*

Sometimes a cubicle-dwelling weasel will become a squatter in a conference room, using it as a surrogate office. He'll drag all of his documents and possessions into the room and set up shop as if there's nothing wrong with it. This is deeply unfair to the weasels that remain behind, festering in cubicles, wishing they had thought of it first. There will be a rush to copy this weasel method, but only the utility closets and bathroom stalls will be left. With weasels, the First Mover Advantage is critical.

One way to circumvent the conference room logjam is to clean out a storage space and make it your department's top-secret hidden meeting room. You might even put a sign on the door that says something deceptive like "Looking for volunteers for a new project. Step right in." Employees will use the outside window ledge to bypass that part of the building.

Weasel Approvals

Over the course of your wretched career it will be necessary to get approval for many work-related things. If done correctly, it is a painful, frustrating, and humiliating experience. That's why you should never do it correctly. The weasel method is the only way to go.

If you work in a large company, try to charge all of your expenses to someone else's project. Usually the accounting and control systems are so poor that no one will notice. If you get caught, say, "Oops," and then start charging your time to someone else's project. This is not yet recognized as a crime. It falls squarely in the weasel zone, and you should exploit it as long as the law allows.

Dear Mr. Adams,

A manager at my company recently confessed that he has never rejected any expense report in his career. The reason is that he does not know how to reject expenses on the on-line system!

There is a bug in my company's expense system that allows the wise weasels to prosper at the expense of lesser weasels. As long as you know the account codes of another group (which are not confidential and you get to know them if you transfer funds even once to/from that group), you can charge any expense to that group and send it for approval to any manager in the company. The group that's getting ripped off never even knows. (With budgets of several million, it is hard to scrutinize a few thousand!)

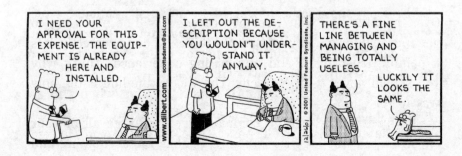

Some people have the motto "It's better to ask forgiveness than to seek approval." Unfortunately, some bosses have the motto "It's better to fire assholes than to deal with them." Make sure your boss doesn't have that motto. The weasel method of asking for forgiveness doesn't work if you do something without permission *and* that something turns out to be a colossal mistake. In that case it's best to multiweasel, i.e., combine two weasel techniques:

1. Act without getting permission
2. Blame someone else for the colossal screwup

Managers who approve things are usually too busy to pay attention to what they are approving. You can make it that much harder by using acronyms and abbreviations. With your naturally unpleasant personality, you can convince people to approve things they don't understand just to spend less time with you.

Employee Recommendations

Intelligence can be measured in several ways. There's the standard IQ (intelligence quotient), which measures math and verbal skills. Then there's the newer EQ (emotional quotient), which measures your ability to postpone satisfaction for a greater gain later. But the most important indicator is the WQ (weasel quotient), a measure of your weasel abilities.

Nowhere is your WQ more important than when you are leaving a job and you are having an "exit interview." The point of an exit interview is for your boss to find out why you are leaving, with an eye toward fixing any problems that you might identify. Someone with a low WQ would answer honestly, sounding something like this: "I've scraped better management skills off the bottom of my sneakers. And on a personal note, you make my skin crawl."

That's all well and good until the time comes when you need a reference for a future employer. A person with a high WQ would recognize the trap and answer this way: "I have learned so much from your leadership that I fear my head will explode if I stay. May I take a picture of you for my wallet?"

A low WQ person generally makes a blunder called altruism.

Altruism: A hallucination that weasels are capable of becoming nonweasels.

During the exit interview, the low WQ person thinks there is an opportunity to make the world a better place. He thinks that by describing the boss's faults to his face some improvements will follow. But it can only end one way:

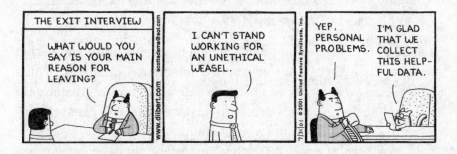

Adaptability

I used to be amazed at media reports of how the typical Japanese worker stayed in the office for twenty-three hours per day, pausing only briefly to slam down a quart of sake, sing karaoke, and pass out in a small, cylindrical bed-hole. This amazing work ethic was the reason for Japan's miraculous economic success.

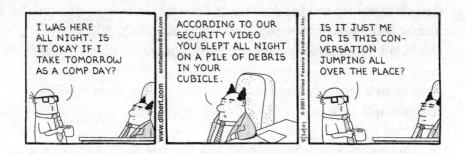

Then one day the Japanese economy got blown away like the origami display at a sumo wrestler's chili festival. I wondered why the great Japanese work ethic wasn't doing its job anymore. Then I learned that Japanese office workers only do "real" work until about six o'clock. After that they spend the next several hours hanging around the office pretending to be busy, saying things to each other like the Japanese version of "So, whatcha up to?"

Okay, I don't know if this version of Japanese office life is true, but it's based on the sort of research I have come to rely on, i.e., overhearing a snippet of a conversation, generalizing it beyond all reasonableness, forgetting the source, and arguing forcefully that it is an established fact.

If you can get past your obsession with reality and focus on my story, it's an excellent example of weaselness gone awry. The Japanese were doing a good job pretending to work—so far, so good—but they failed to update their weasel techniques to keep up with the times. That is where American workers excel. We can sniff out a weasel opportunity years in advance and adapt instantly.

When the dotcom bubble started forming in the midnineties, it generated a weasel feeding frenzy. It was as if the gods of commerce had inexplicably said, "For one day only, it's okay to steal." All you had to do was convince some sucker to buy the stock that you had bought from some other sucker. This system worked well for the weasels with the best timing. They did their stealing and scampered out of town with huge truckloads of unearned cash.

The moral of this story—and yes there is one—is that you shouldn't be sleeping in cylindrical bed-holes when you could be scampering out of town with huge truckloads of other people's money.

Thwarting the Rules

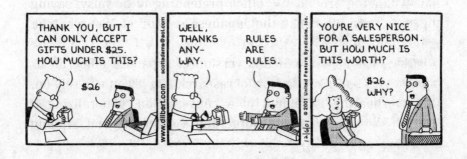

In a corporation, every time someone does something dumb or unethical, a new rule springs up to keep it from happening again. Luckily there is no end to how clever the average weasel can be, so rules don't slow anyone down.

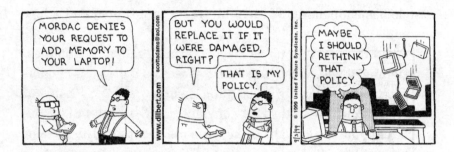

Rule-breaking is such a popular activity that it has its own little motto: "Rules are made to be broken." This clever saying is right up there with other all-time great sayings including "People were meant to be punched" and "Cars were meant to be driven by drunks." Someday I'd like to see a televised trial of a serial killer whose lawyer sums up his case, "Hey, rules are made to be broken." The jurors would probably say, "Why didn't he say that in the first place?" and "Good point."

If you have the sort of job that requires tracking your time so it can be billed, you have the ultimate weasel situation. First of all, if there were any way to independently verify how you allocate your time, then you wouldn't have to keep a time card. That means you're home free to "use your judgment" in the ambiguous situations. For example, if you're traveling in your car to a meeting for one customer while talking on the phone to another, you can bill whichever one you hate the most. Or you can bill both. You can even bill a third client that you were thinking about.

You can also get paid for making small talk. When you walk into a meeting with a client, the meter is running no matter what you talk about. There's no reason to engage in tiresome conversations about work when you can get paid for blabbing about the weather and who had the flu recently and whether a new hairstyle has enough highlights.

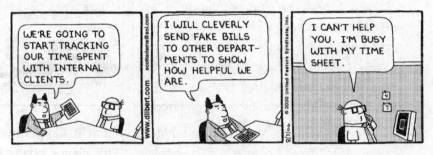

For every tracking system invented by management there is some weasel way of thwarting it. Here's a good example.

Dear Mr. Adams,

Management just sent this e-mail:
"In order to kick off Waste Reduction Week we have been challenged to reduce the use of Styrofoam cups. We will have new bags placed in the recycle bin areas on Monday and at the end of the day check to see which department used the fewest cups. We can all be winners here!"

It was immediately obvious that we could win the "fewest cups" challenge by discarding our Styrofoam cups in the regular garbage instead of the recycling bag.

Here's a test of your weasel quotient. Read the following e-mail and figure out how you would thwart this company policy.

> Dear Mr. Adams,
>
> The IT department told one of my coworkers that she would have to turn in her old computer before a new machine could be ordered for her. They won't even put in the paperwork until they have the old computer. So for two to six weeks she will have no computer at all while waiting for the new machine.
>   When she questioned the IT guy about the logic of this, he said, "I know it doesn't make any sense, but that's the policy."

The correct solution is to wait until the person who hatched the computer replacement policy is out of the office. Then take his computer and turn it in to IT.

Some aggressive companies have a rule that every year the worst 10 percent of the performers in the company have to be fired. I've never worked at one of those companies, but I don't need a crystal ball to know what kind of weasel fight that kicks off every year. I assume that every department manager agrees that there is plenty of deadwood in the company but argues that it's in other departments. Failing in that argument, the manager has to make one of his employees seem extra incompetent so the firing doesn't seem random. So if you work in a small department of, say, four people, your boss is actively plotting someone's demise. And you know what that means: any time you spend not bad-mouthing your coworkers is time wasted.

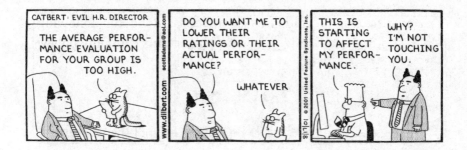

The only thing worse than a weasel is a motivated weasel. That's why it's never a good idea to give incentives of any kind to weasels. You might as well throw a lighted match into a barrel of gasoline. The only thing that keeps society intact is that weasels are diluted across lots of different situations. Here's an example of what happens when weasels are focused on a specific goal.

Dear Mr. Adams,

I travel a lot to Asia. I've always wondered why *every* trip seems to require going through Tokyo or Osaka. This is especially weird on the flights to Hong Kong and Seoul where direct nonstop flights are available. Recently I discovered the reason: our company travel agents—who are company employees—get bonuses based on booking to our two most popular destinations, which just happen to be Tokyo and Osaka. Flights to other cities don't count for as many "bonus points." Nice little system, huh?

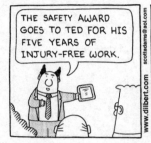
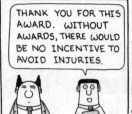
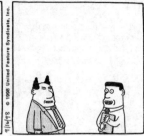

4

Headcount Weasels

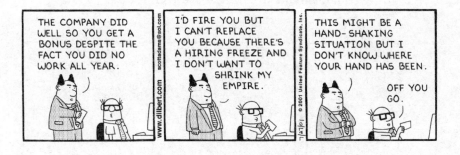

When you join a company, you can choose to be a hardworking superstar employee (I don't recommend it) or you can take the Way of the Weasel and accept that you are a "headcount."

As a headcount you are essential to supporting the quality of your boss's furniture. The more headcount he manages, the better furniture he's allowed to have. Your primary job is to stay on the payroll and spend as little of the budget as possible.

When your boss is negotiating with his boss for better office furniture—that's when your existence matters. He'll say something to the effect of "Look at all the headcount I have! I can't manage all that headcount from a little chair!"

A good headcount knows how to avoid doomed projects, thus

improving the odds of staying on the payroll. You can identify a doomed project by any of these telltale signs:

1. It was a pet project of an executive who just left the company.

2. The project manager uses words like *space* and *architecture* a lot.

3. The team members are people like you.

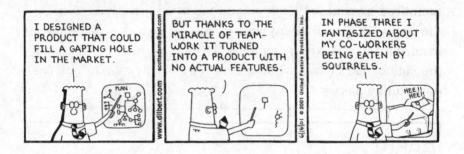

There are only two kinds of projects—(1) growing and (2) doomed. If a project isn't adding people, taking over new cubicles, having more meetings, and expanding its budget, it's doomed. All the smart weasels will defect to the growing project, leaving the lesser weasels to turn out the lights on the loser project. Don't be a lesser weasel if you can avoid it.

It's okay to earn raises, but don't allow yourself to be the highest-paid weasel in the department even if you deserve it. The highest paid are often the first to be downsized, freeing the most budget money for your boss's furniture. If you happen to accidentally do a spectacular job, thus risking a large pay increase, pull back on the reins a bit. Let a few deadlines slip, overspend, slap a customer—whatever it takes.

Don't be a complainer either. If your neck is severed in an industrial accident and your head rolls down the hall and into your boss's office, keep a cheery look on your face and wait for someone to kick your head back into the hall. You don't want your boss to look at you every day and think, "Oh, there's that headcount who's always causing me trouble."

Someday I hope someone will invent camouflage clothing that looks like cubicle walls. That way you'll be able to move unnoticed around the office. If you see your boss walking down the hall with paper of any sort in his hand, he's looking for a headcount to give an assignment to. You'll want to dissolve into the side of the nearest cubicle and remain motionless until the opportunity passes.

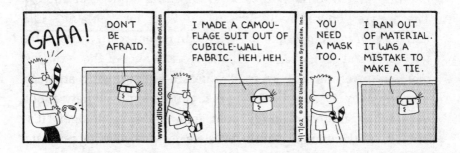

The more experienced headcounts will learn to make the least amount of disruption in the environment. Try to walk sideways so you don't displace much air. Avoid perfumes, lotions, colognes, and microwave popcorn. Turn down the sound on your computer and turn off your telephone ringer. Do what the submarine captains do—run silent, run deep.

If you absolutely have to walk down the hall, try to slip behind a plus-size headcount who is heading in the same direction. Use him or her as cover to move from one place to the other like a dolphin following a cruise ship.

If, despite all your stealthy practices, you are given an assignment, never argue with its objectives no matter how ridiculous. Moreover, never do anything that puts you at risk of accomplishing the objectives, because that attracts attention. Your best bet is to continually seek information, attend meetings off-site, and later redefine the scope of the project so it's not obvious you've never completed anything.

Pick the Right Company

If your company sells a product that people need, there's almost nothing you can do to stop them from trying to give you money. That's a very liberating thought. Try to work for companies that make essential things like electricity and clean water and cable television and phone service. If you work in one of those places, you don't even have to pretend you care about your customers. The only way it could be better is if you had special permission to punch customers who deserved it. And that's not as hard to arrange as you might think, because given a choice of losing electricity or taking a sock in the gut, most people would take the punch.

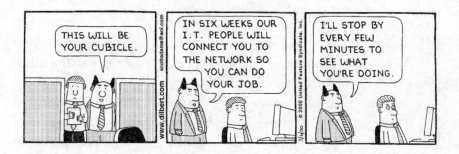

If you follow this advice, you will have a long and unproductive career that does absolutely nothing to help future generations, who—as you know—have done nothing to help you.

Hiding Your Incompetence

If you are colossally incompetent at your job, it's a good idea to keep that fact to yourself. The three most potent cloaking tools of the incompetent weasel are:

1. Getting angry
2. Talking during meetings
3. Acting overworked

You can make timid people stop asking questions by answering the wrong question and then acting angry that your answer is not being treated as if it's adequate. When faced with this tactic, most timid victims will give up and look for something else to do.

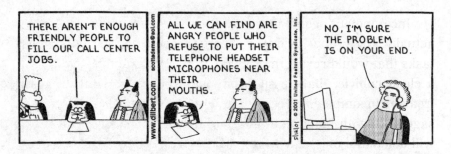

In meetings, the person who is least competent usually does the most talking. Talking is a direct substitute for competence, at least in the minds of other people. Five minutes after you leave a meeting, you won't remember what anyone said but you will remember who did most of the talking. Within a day your mind will translate that into a notion that the talker was unusually knowledgeable.

I know that sounds crazy but here's an analogy from the restaurant business. Studies have shown* that what people remember most about a dining experience is the *size of the portions*. It's the same thing with meetings: the more you talk, the more valuable you seem.

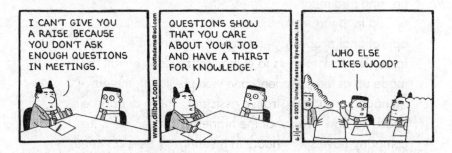

*When I say "studies have shown," that means I heard it from someone who heard it from someone. The original study was probably about dolphin migration patterns.

Incompetent people like to fill their schedule with things they actually know how to do so they can avoid more challenging tasks that would reveal their true nature. For example, if you see a clean cubicle, that's a sign that the occupant is either a neat freak or incompetent. To find out which, leave a voice mail message asking an inane and unimportant question. The neat freak will delete the message just to get the voice mailbox cleaned out, then ignore you to reduce the later risk of shaking your infected hand. The incompetent employee will seize the opportunity to work on something that is as easy as it is unimportant. He'll call you right back and offer to set up a meeting.

Dear Mr. Adams,

In my company it is nearly impossible to get people in other departments to do their jobs. Most of the managers spend their time trying to blame other departments for problems instead of actually working. Despite all this, sales are way up, and that magnifies all the other issues.

So in the face of all the extra work and major operational problems, management has formed a task force. The task force is to eliminate frivolous e-mail. It's made up of the president, one vice president, the office manager, an administrative assistant, and a department head. So now several of the highest-paid people in the company have spent hours in meetings to develop three pages of rules on when e-mails should and shouldn't be sent and what should be included in them.

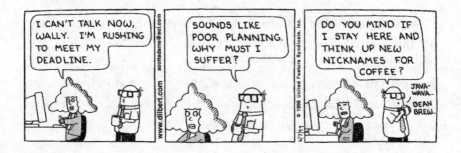

Sycophant*

Sucking up to the boss is a time-honored weasel tradition and an excellent way to keep your job. The technique has been around for a long time. I'm guessing it started at the dawn of humanity when the first cave person said to his tribal leader, "You make good fire. Ogg could never make fire that good. Your club is huge."

Thanks to evolution, humans made the leap from sniffing butts to kissing butts, and the seeds of capitalism were sown.

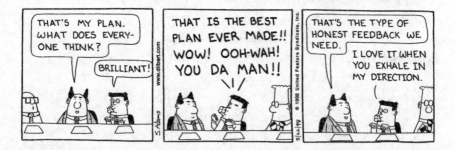

The great thing about being a sycophant is that there's no deception going on. You know you're a weasel, your boss knows

*This is the fancy word for a butt-kissing, suck-up weasel.

you're a weasel, and your coworkers know you're a weasel. And yet, the method still works like a charm. As a flatterer, you're competing for your boss's affections against people who are disgruntled whiners. You could be the most heinous sycophant in the world and still win that competition. When it's time to downsize, is your boss going to get rid of the person who says, "Your hair is excellent and your judgment is even better," or the one who says, "If I fail because of budget cuts, I'm telling everyone it was your fault"?

Dear Mr. Adams,

Our company changed its name and had a meeting to announce the new name. Our CEO was answering questions from the employees and wanted to check with one of his VPs in the back of the room to see if he had anything to add to the answer the CEO had just given. The VP said, "I think what you think."

Forecasting

When you lie about the future, that's called optimism, and it is considered a virtue. Technically speaking you can't "lie" about the future because no one knows what will happen. When you apply this unique brand of optimism (not lying!) at work, that's called forecasting.

If your job burdens you with something called "knowledge," then you probably have people bugging you to predict the future of sales or expenses or market share or employee injuries or what have you. That's when you need to do some forecasting to get them off your back.

Forecasting: A method invented by weasels to make people stop asking questions.

If someone asks you about the future, avoid responding with the truth, as in "How the %@$% should I know the future? Do you see an eye in the middle of my forehead?" The truth won't make anyone stop asking questions. It might even attract a crowd of curious onlookers, and that works against your goal of being an invisible headcount.

A better approach is to say, "Sales will be exactly $376.83 million in 12 months." When people hear a confident forecast like that, they leave your cubicle and get on to the important business of misinterpreting what you said and forgetting that you exist.

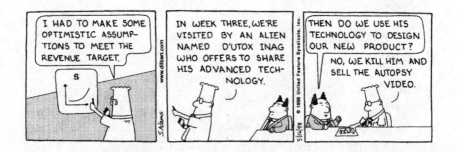

The thing to remember about forecasts is that no one expects you to be accurate. So there's no need to knock yourself out with meaningless tasks such as gathering data or thinking before you speak. In the unlikely event that someone later compares your forecast to reality and finds no correlation, blame the weather.*

You can blame almost anything on the weather. Don't be limited to the obvious stuff like changes in fuel consumption, construction, and shopping levels. It doesn't matter if your product is a beverage made of turpentine—you can still blame the weather for a slump in sales. And don't limit yourself to using *bad* weather as your excuse. Good weather can hurt sales too. If it's sunny and warm, you can say people didn't buy your turpentine beverage because they were on vacation. If it's cold and snowy, you can say they didn't want to leave the house to go to the store to buy your turpentine beverage.

No one believes forecasts, but we all want to hear them. Your brain is like your stomach in the sense that if it's empty, you're willing to put anything in there to fill it up. If you're nervous or curious about the future, then whatever you hear next, no matter how many "ifs" are involved, you'll hear it as a fact.

Example:

What is said: If war breaks out between Switzerland and Sweden and there's a shortage of rubber and someone invents a way to turn turpentine beverages into tires, and all the other turpentine manufacturers go out of business at once, we could sell

---

*Unless you are a weather forecaster. In that case you should blame a high-pressure system from the north, which is another way of blaming the weather, but it sounds less ironic.

> two million cases of our soft drink
> sometime during the next century.

> Fact you hear: We're selling two million cases. No
> doubt about it.

Ideally, when the future arrives and your forecast is revealed for the steaming load of fertilizer that it is, you want to have someone else to blame. If the forecast involves a slipped schedule, you can find yourself in a pitched contest called Schedule Chicken, like this:

Dear Mr. Adams,

I'm working as a contractor at a company that I shouldn't name, and they have a phenomenon called Schedule Chicken. The project has three software managers, and each one knows the schedule is slipping. Each one has dozens of red flags that show they can't ship. The managers come up with ridiculous reasons why they will be able to fix the red flags in time, so they won't be blamed as the one to cause a change in the ship date. The losing manager is the one that finally can't take the pressure anymore and asks management to slip the ship date. Then the other two managers take a gasp breath of relief and say that they might also be able to use some extra time.

Sometimes a weasel will get cornered by a higher-level weasel and be forced to confess his sins. This is never attractive, as you can see in this example:

Dear Mr. Adams,

Our boss had to meet with his superiors to discuss the status of our project. The project was behind schedule but our boss was not planning to admit this. Prior to the meeting, one of the vice presidents had found out the schedule was going to slip. He asked our boss point-blank if our project was going to meet the deadline. My boss replied that it was. The VP said he had it on good authority that the project schedule would slip by three months, therefore our boss must be either incompetent or a liar.

Our boss shot back immediately, "I am not incompetent!"

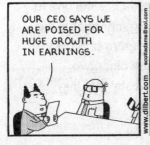
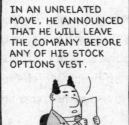
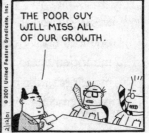

Company Cults

Your company might be a cult. That can be good because in terms of blending into the background it doesn't get any easier. Your company will tell you exactly how to behave in order to be indistinguishable from every other headcount. So even if you make the mistake of being noticed by management, someone else will probably get blamed for whatever you screwed up.

One way to find out if your company is a cult is to see if you have a "values statement." A values statement describes how the employees are expected to act and includes things like honesty, trust, and teamwork. A values statement is created when managers realize their entire staff is infested with weasels. Weasel infestation is a huge problem for senior management because it greatly reduces the assets of the company that are available for them to steal via a process known as stock options. The popular management antidote to weasel infestation is a subtle form of brainwashing using posters and paperweights. This works wonders on the more gullible segment of the weasel population. And that's a bigger segment than you might think. For every nut that runs off and joins a cult there are five other nuts that just ba-a-a-arely resisted, and only because they don't look good in robes. Those people work for big corporations and rely on the values statement to keep them from pillaging.

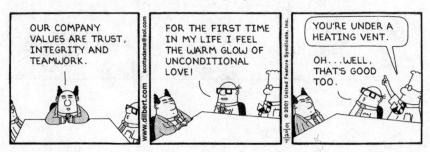

In fact, companies are borrowing more techniques from cults every day. For example, cults try to separate you from the rest of society. Companies make you work so many hours that you never see the rest of society. Cults tell you to wear dorky outfits. Companies tell you to wear dorky outfits too, except on casual day, when they tell you to wear *casual* dorky outfits. Cults make you give them all your money. Companies make you give them all of your ideas, inventions, and patents. Cults make you chant. Companies make you answer the phone the same way every time. Cults teach you to clear your mind of all thoughts. Companies make you attend meetings. Coincidence?

If you suspect that your company has become a cult, don't be alarmed unless you hear any of the red flag phrases such as *comet, Kool-Aid, polygamy, shaved head,* and *multilevel marketing.*

5

Motivating Like a Weasel

Being a midlevel manager is like being a fisherman, except instead of having an efficient fishing tool, such as a fishing pole or a net or dynamite, you have to talk the fish into surrendering. Sometimes a flying fish will accidentally jump into your boat, at which point you can write a bestselling management book about it. The rest of the time you end up shouting slogans about teamwork and excellence into the water and hoping for the best.

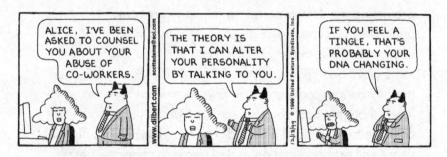

A manager has to be a motivator because self-motivated employees are rare. How rare, you ask?

Imagine the abominable snowman milking the Loch Ness monster to get milk for his pet unicorn. Self-motivated employees are more rare than good analogies in this book.

Motivating isn't easy. It's inconvenient to fire an employee because then you have to hire a new one and beat the creativity out of it, also known as "training." Employees know you're too lazy to do that sort of thing often, so the threat of getting fired doesn't motivate them.

And you can't offer big raises to employees because the budget is tight. So money doesn't motivate them. The only motivational tools at your disposal are ones that frankly make no sense. For example . . .

From the e-mail bag:

> Dear Mr. Adams,
>
> I have worked at my employer for a year and had my first review yesterday. The review was fantastic, and my boss informed me that she was pleased to announce that she was promoting me. However, apparently my company underwent a secret reorganization last year. None of the employees knew about it. Apparently I was demoted at some point and never notified. So in my review my boss happily announced that I have been promoted back to the level I thought I had always been at! Yippee. I figure if I continue to work hard and dedicate myself to my job, next year I will probably get promoted again to my current level.

Imaginary Raises

If your budget won't allow you to give real raises to your employees, the next best thing is giving imaginary raises. This method is increasingly popular, owing to its extreme cost-effectiveness.

Imaginary raises come in several forms. The first type involves informing employees what they would have gotten as a raise if in fact there had been any money in the budget for that sort of thing.

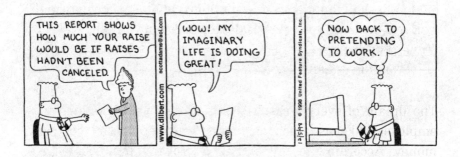

The next type of imaginary raise involves gathering data to show that your employees are already highly paid compared to people someplace else. That can make the employees feel wealthier without costing you a penny.

Example:

      Boss: You're highly paid compared to the mud peo-
                ple of the lower Amazon. Their annual bonus
                is a back-scratcher made from a kangaroo's
                rib.
Employee: I think you have your continents mixed up.
      Boss: Sheeesh. I try to meet you halfway and all you
                do is complain.

Things That Are As Good As Money

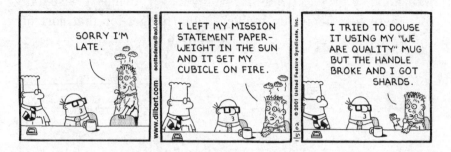

The dream of every weasel boss is to discover something that employees like as much as money and yet doesn't cost any money. According to my e-mail, a growing trend is to give employees rocks.

Dear Mr. Adams,

Last spring I happily organized a clothing drive at work. We collected nearly three tons of clothes for the needy.

For my good work I received a present from the corporate Community Relations people. It's a rock with the word *inspiration* carved into it. The box has a few paragraphs on it: "What is a rock besides a naturally formed mineral from the crust of the earth?" And goes on, "You act upon inspiration that makes our community and world a better place."

That would be just fine if the rock was really a rock. But I guess they're hard to find these days. So they sent me a rock that's plastic.

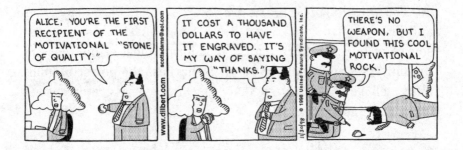

Dear Mr. Adams,

We low-level managers attended a meeting to learn that after the layoffs we carry the burden for motivating the workforce back into an energized and newly productive state.

One of the suggestions for rewarding people without money was to create colored three-by-five cards with words like *commitment* and *good job* or *extra effort,* and when someone demonstrates one of these qualities, give him a card. It was hypothesized that soon people would be focusing on how to get the most three-by-five cards. One manager raised his hand and said that he apologized for being cynical, but if he gave out three-by-five cards to his staff, they would laugh themselves into hernias and he would lose all credibility. Someone suggested he use larger cards.

The only thing less expensive and more abundant than rocks and three-by-five cards is gullibility. Some physicists say it's the source of invisible dark matter that forms most of the mass of the universe, and I believe them. To harness the power of gullibility, tell your employees that they are working for reasons other than money, i.e., imaginary reasons.

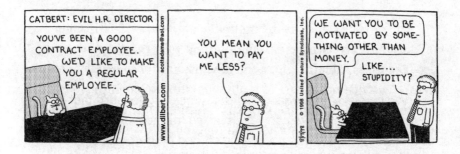

It can also be helpful to compare your employees to imaginary employees. The imaginary employees are able to work amazingly long hours without the need for sleep or food or personal relationships. Imaginary people are the best role models.

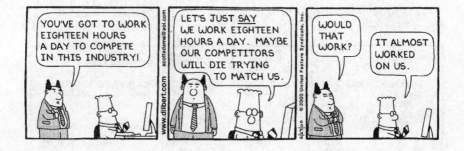

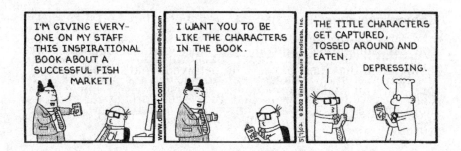

An inexpensive way to motivate employees is through pep talks. There are two types. One method tells the employees they are worthless slackers and need to work harder in order to justify their existence on earth. The other method tells employees they are the best in the entire industry despite what their paychecks say. You can never be sure which method will work best for your employees, so it's a good idea to try both and see what happens.

> ***Boss***:   You are the best workers on earth!
>
> ***Employee***:   Suddenly I'm feeling listless. What the hell just happened?
>
> ***Boss***:   I meant to say you're all lazy and worthless! I should fire you right now!
>
> ***Employee***:   Wow! I just felt a surge of energy. Thanks!

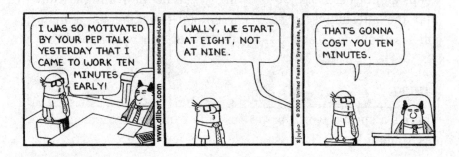

Competitive Pay

You can sometimes motivate the more gullible employees by telling them that their pay is "competitive." That's another word for "You can make more money someplace else," but it's far more motivating. Motivating has a lot to do with your choice of words.

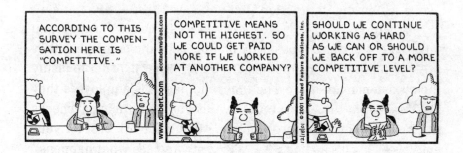

Job Interviews

Luckily for managers everywhere, the most dreaded experience in the life of any employee is the job interview. Most employees prefer years of abuse over job interviews. There is a sort of informal cartel agreement among all companies to make the interview process as humiliating and degrading as possible. That keeps employees from job-hopping. It can be motivating to know that the alternative to your current job—looking for a better job—is about as pleasant as combing your hair with a feral cat.

Caring

There's a special word for bosses who care about their employees: unemployed. The whole point of being a boss is to get employees to do more work than they want to do and to accept less pay than they deserve. If a boss starts caring about employees, it screws up the whole oppressor-victim dynamic of capitalism. That's where weasel-caring comes in. It's similar to real caring but without any of the ill effects. For example, you might assign one of your employees to organize a potluck lunch for the department. It costs you nothing in either money or productivity while giving the impression that you care. Best of all, you get a free lunch.

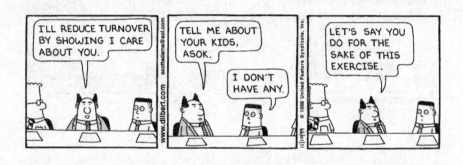

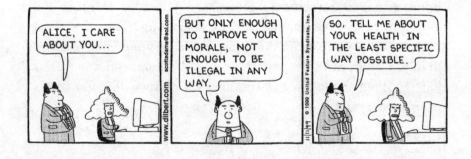

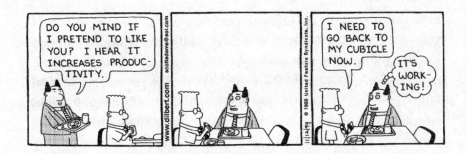

A close relative of weasel-caring is weasel-listening. The point of weasel-listening is to act as if you value the input of other people.

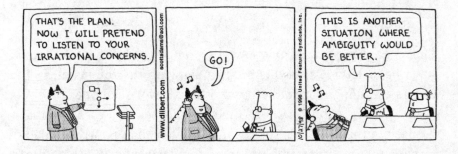

Being Like a Little Person

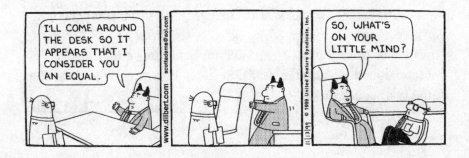

If you're a stinkin' rich executive, your employees might resent you. You'll need to pretend to be like a little person in some ways to reduce the hatred.

One popular method for acting like a little person is to move out of your big office and into a cubicle. That sends the message "If I can work in a tiny cubicle without complaining, then so can you."

That might seem like a big sacrifice to you. But if you're earning $200 million a year, own four mansions and a yacht, commute by helicopter, and have a high-priced call girl for a secretary—that will take the sting out of sitting in a cubicle.

Slogans

Slogans are important for motivating employees. I'm sure there have been lots of scientific studies showing the importance of slogans, although for some reason I have never seen one.

Managers should exhort their employees to work with a "sense of urgency." This sounds much better than poorly worded slogans that mean exactly the same thing, such as "Work with a constant feeling of unnecessary stress" or "If it didn't hurt so much, I wouldn't need to pay you to do it."

Common sense tells you that slogans do in fact improve the quality of work in your group. During the time you are reading the slogan from a poster, you will not be doing something that is potentially even stupider, and that in itself can raise the average quality of your work.

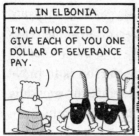
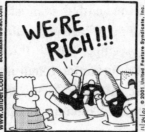
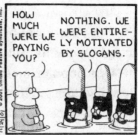

Dear Mr. Adams,

My new general manager plastered around the office the following phrase in an attempt to motivate us to greatness. It's really annoying. The phrase:
  "How do we get it done? By doing it!"
He has another too:
  "We already are what others hope to be."

When concocting your motivational slogan, make sure the staff can't change a word or two and make it sound funny. When I worked at Pacific Bell, the corporate slogan was "Good enough isn't!" Within minutes of the rollout we had warped the slogan to "Good enough is!" and used it several times a day. The normal context was something like this:

> ***Me:*** Here are those numbers you asked for. I didn't have accurate information so I just used the numbers from my license plate.
>
> ***Coworker:*** Good enough is.
>
> ***Me:*** You got that right.

It's always a good idea to tell your employees that they are the best workers in the world despite all evidence to the contrary. This is another example where the Way of the Weasel is best for everyone concerned. The truth would be somewhat demotivating, sounding like this: "Our employees are slightly below average because all the good ones left for better jobs."

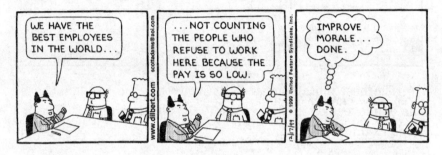

Morale Boosting

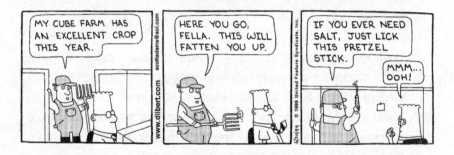

You can compensate for low pay by increasing the morale of your employees. In theory, you can make your employees so happy they will pay you for the privilege of working. But there's no need to overdo it. All you have to do is improve moral enough to close the gap between what you pay the employees and what they could get at some other job that sucks just as much. That's where morale-boosting activities come in.

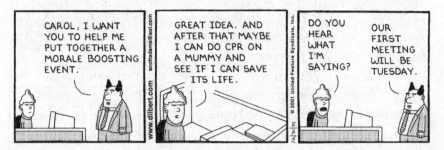

The best morale-boosting activities are the ones that make the employees do all the work and, ideally, foot the bill. Here's a good example.

Dear Mr. Adams,

I wanted to tell you about a "scheme" my company has come up with to raise the morale of the employees. We have been subject to cost containment for many months. The VP of our company came up with an idea that we would decorate all of our offices and compete against each other for creativity, attitude, and willingness to participate. After making many plans and getting excited, we all found out that we must pay for any decorations or provisions we need. Who ever heard of paying for your own morale??? To top it off, we were told that anything we did in relationship to this "contest" would have to be done on our own time, meaning after hours. So now not only do we have to pay for our own morale, we have to do it on our time.

Noble Rationale

If something is good for your employees, then there's no reason to make it sound nobler than it really is. For example, if you want to give them more money, you can say, "Here's a raise." It's a simple and clear message.

The time to get fancy is when you want to save money in some way that ends up screwing your employees. In those situations you want to use noble language, like "we need to improve communication" or "increase creativity" or "improve customer service." Employees will eventually learn to predict the degree of screwing they're going to get by counting the number of syllables it takes to reassure them everything is okay. But they'll still appreciate that you made an effort to dress it up.

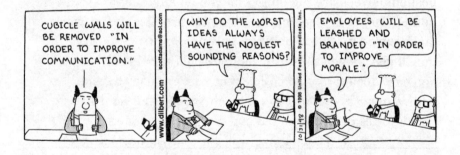

Let's say you wanted to sell all your cubicle walls and office furniture and make the employees sit on the floor all day. You could put a positive spin on it by pointing out how it increases communication. Most of that increase will be in the form of plotting revenge, but you don't have to dwell on the negative.

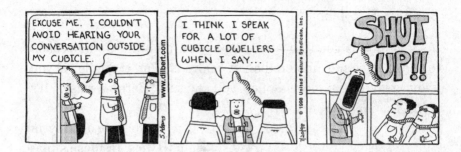

Employee Egos

You want the egos of your employees to be healthy enough to keep their cellular structure from premature rotting, yet weak enough that they don't go looking for a better job. That's why the best kind of work environment is a mildly dysfunctional one that's just *barely* better than the employees' personal lives. The best employees are the ones who will do anything to avoid going home. They'll be seeking comfort and gratification at work. So make sure you don't give them any comfort or gratification or they'll get hooked on the feeling and become needy and whiny. You can't please dysfunctional people; it's like drying your hands with water.

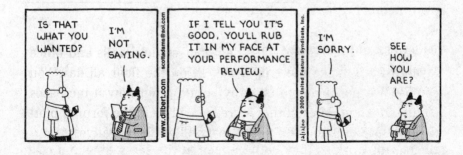

Business Enjoyment

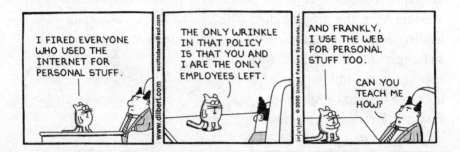

An observant boss will take time from his morale-boosting activities to yell at the employees for having fun during work. It sounds like this:

"Stop using the Internet for personal use."

"Stop chatting with coworkers."

"Stop eating at your desk."

Those forbidden activities generate "actual enjoyment," and as a manager you want to replace it with something called "business enjoyment" whenever possible. Business enjoyment is the only kind of joy that is approved by your company.

Business enjoyment: A form of enjoyment experienced in the workplace that uses no company resources and includes no enjoyment.

Ideally you want your employees to interlace business enjoyment with work so they both happen at the same time and cost the company nothing. For example, it would be inappropriate to interrupt a meeting to tell a joke that's off the topic. That's like stealing from the stockholders. But you can comically refer to a leading-edge project as a "bleeding edge" project and laugh in a self-conscious way that makes everyone want to slap you. That takes no extra time and it lends an air of frivolity to an otherwise lifeless meeting. Your employees might have so much fun that they ask for a cut in pay to keep things fair.

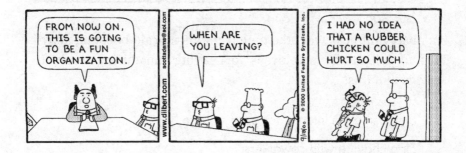

Your goal is to convince your employees that the mind-numbing drudgery they call "work" can be loads of fun if they just change their attitudes. If you plop a four-hour assignment on a subordinate's desk at 6 P.M.—an assignment that you've known about for weeks—usually the employee will pantomime your strangulation as soon as you turn your back. That's no good. You want employees who are so happy—preferably for no good reason—that they offer you a mint and a foot massage every time you walk past. If they just loosen up a bit, they can have a good laugh at your habitual callousness and incompetence. Your employee might even say to you, "You're a piece of work!" and you'll respond, "There's no bout a doubt it." Then the two of you will share a hearty company-approved laugh.

Dear Mr. Adams,

While interviewing for a telephone customer-service position for a mortgage company, one of the vice presidents told me that they make an effort to create a "real fun" atmosphere at work. When I pressed for a specific example, she said that sometimes, when employees have had to answer calls for several hours straight, they let the employees switch to doing filing. I waited for the punch line, but alas, there was none.

6

Manager Weasels

Doing Something

As a manager, all of your information comes from your employees. And they're all notorious weasels. That means 99 percent of the time you have no idea what the real problem is or what needs to be done. Whatever you decide to do is likely to fall into the random category. But you must do *something*—i.e., act like a manager—or else a better actor will replace you. The best solution is to do something ridiculous and hope you can convince people you're being creative. Later when everything goes into the dumper, you can always brag about your innovative spirit. Here's an example:

> Dear Mr. Adams,
>
> Today wasn't a good day. The Service Center people were already a bit edgy because of a recent worldwide ATM outage. Then, about 9 A.M., the network starts to crap out. Phone reps can't get to their systems. Calls get backed up.
> Then an announcement says there's no water to the buildings. We're told to stay out of the rest rooms. And

since the water was out, that meant the air-conditioning was out too, since it requires water. It started getting hot in here.

Then management made what I call one of their power decisions . . .

They sent in the clowns.

I'm going to repeat that, as it bears repeating.

They *sent* *in* *the* *clowns.*

No, I'm not referring to senior management. Those clowns would never come down here.

I'm talking about *real* clowns. Management went out and hired a troop of floppy-shoed, white-faced, red-nosed, mop-haired, horn-tooting drama-class dropouts to come in and "entertain the troops."

So, let me recap: network out, temperature unbearable, no water, no rest rooms, phone calls backed up, chaos everywhere you look. And clowns roaming the building.

But the clowns did have an effect on morale. You had to laugh at the fact that the best solution our management could come up with was to HIRE CLOWNS.

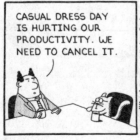
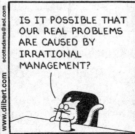
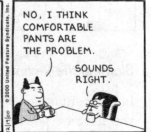

Humiliating Assignments

As a boss, sometimes you need to assign degrading and humiliating tasks to members of your staff, either because the tasks need to get done or sometimes just for fun. Your easiest solution is to give the humiliating assignment to the youngest person. Young people expect to get crapped on. They're still naive enough to think that teamwork and dedication will help their career. You could say to a twenty-two-year-old, "Climb down that sewer hole and squeeze all the rats to see if any coins come out." The next sound you'd hear would be a splash.

Eventually young employees grow up to be bitter and cynical skin-covered vehicles used to transport bile from one meeting to another. But until then, they are valuable resources. It might be necessary to tell your young employees that an assignment is more important than it really is, as in this example.

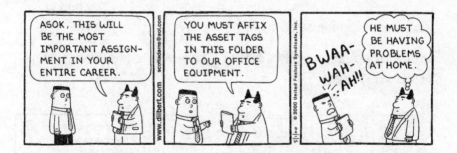

Blaming the Victim

In most situations it's easy to blame the victim for whatever evil you have perpetrated, e.g., "He darted into the crosswalk, Officer!" But for years, managers had no easy way to blame employees for their own bad management. That's when someone had the bright idea to invent the word *empowerment*.

The idea behind empowerment is that employees were authorized to make their own decisions, but only if those decisions were the same ones the boss would have made. In practice, this is exactly like giving the employees no authority whatsoever with the added advantage that you can punish them for not reading your mind.

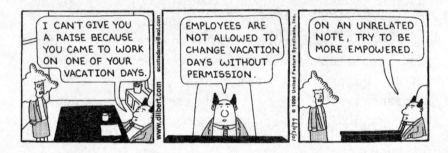

Keeping Priorities Straight

From my e-mail, here is a tale of a boss who knew how to keep priorities straight.

> Dear Mr. Adams,
>
> I am a paramedic, and this really happened.
>
> I responded to an ambulance call for a man having a heart attack. When we got to the scene, the man appeared stable. It was a real heart attack but the man wasn't knocking on death's door. Before we could even get him out

of his office, his VP shoved papers under his nose to sign. Then the boss asked us to take the victim's briefcase and laptop to the emergency room so he could continue to work on a project. His secretary told him he had a call holding and asked him if she should take a number, or did he want to take the call right then, or should she forward it to his cell phone so he could talk while en route to the ER. Finally, as we were rolling him out the door, I overheard a coworker say, "If he doesn't come back, I'm calling dibs on his office."

He recovered from the heart attack, but I don't know if he'll survive the office.

Stealth Firing

Sometimes you need to fire employees for good reasons including but not limited to:

1. They seem creepy.
2. You haven't seen them steal but you think they might.
3. There's something in their tone of voice that you don't like.

Obviously you want to generate some sort of weasel "reason" that sounds better than the real reason or else there will be no end to the whining. The best approach is to create an environment where the employee is doomed to job failure. Here's how one boss handled that tricky situation.

Dear Mr. Adams,

I was a project coordinator (meaning I had all of the responsibility and none of the authority) and I shared a secretary with a few other coworkers. Each time I'd ask the secretary to do something for me, she would have a tantrum and insist that it was NOT her job. It wasn't until we had to get a mediator that I discovered that the pointy-haired boss had intentionally given us conflicting versions of the secretary's job description in order to create a conflict so he could fire me.

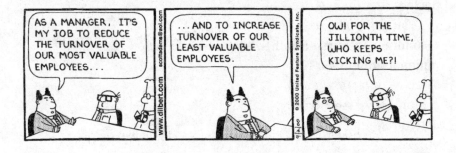

Another popular method for weeding out undesirable employees is the "bad assignment." Give the undesirable employee a project that is as unpleasant as it is unnecessary. Ideally the task will be one that has ruined a few careers already. Your smarter victims will get the message and immediately resign to "pursue other opportunities." The more stubborn weeds will dig in their heels and counter your weasel move with a full arsenal of weasel countermeasures. But time is on your side. Slowly increase the pressure by relocating cubicles until your victim is surrounded on three sides by these coworkers:*

1. A guy who uses his speakerphone all day long.

2. A woman who applies perfume with a fog machine.

3. Someone with an annoying and continuous high-pitched laugh.

The riskiest way to fire someone is by telling the truth, e.g., "Ted, you are a lazy and worthless weasel. I am firing you because I can't stand to look at your face." That's just asking for trouble. The safest way to jettison an unwanted employee is to declare that the job has become "redundant."

You can make a job redundant in several ways. One method is to hire an additional weasel and give the new weasel the same duties as the targeted employee but under a different job title. Then wait a few months and fire the first weasel for being redundant. Unfortunately that's expensive because there is actual redundancy involved. Here's a better method.

Dear Mr. Adams,

On my third day at a new job, a coworker took me aside and explained various ways to look like I'm working when

*This is the same strategy the CIA used to get Manuel Noriega out of Panama.

I'm not. A few weeks later her position was eliminated because of "redundancy." Apparently the pointy-haired boss feared a lawsuit if he fired her outright. So to prove she was redundant he gave me all her work in addition to my own. My new position was paid less than the eliminated position, even though it had twice the responsibility. My boss said he had to do that to justify to human resources how I was not redundant.

Stealing Employees

When you move to a management job at a new company, you might be tempted to hire some of the better employees from your old company. But chances are that you signed an employment agreement with your prior company that says you won't solicit its employees after you leave. That's a big problem for an ethical person who observes the intent of agreements. But it's no obstacle for a weasel.

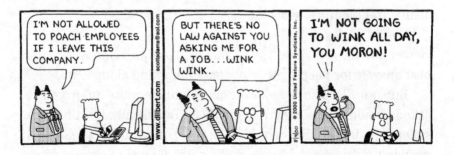

Instead of actively "soliciting" employees of your old company, just call the ones you want and tell them how wonderful the new company is. Mention the excellent pay and unusually gifted management team. Say how sorry you feel for the people you left behind. Unless the employee has the intellect of yeast, he or she will start asking you about openings. And that's totally legal because you didn't solicit, it "just happened."

Selective Truth

The best way to mislead people without lying is to avoid volunteering unpleasant truths. Technically, that's not lying.

> Dear Mr. Adams,
>
> My boss is a king weasel. He doesn't lie to customers; he calls it "nonfull disclosure."

Don't feel bad about nonfull disclosure. It's a public service. If people knew what they were buying or eating or whom they were hiring, then no one would do anything, the economy would disintegrate, and we'd all starve to death.

For example, if you were applying for a job and the interviewer asked, "Have you ever stolen from an employer?" the best answer for keeping the economy humming along is no.

But full disclosure, where you volunteer more than you're asked, would look something like this: "Technically, no, I haven't stolen yet. But I fantasize about it a lot. I'm afraid of jail so I wouldn't steal unless I had a really good chance of getting away with it. I mean, if you give me a clear opening, I'm going for it, especially if you start jacking me around. Because then you'll deserve it."

Thickheadedness

Thickheadedness, either real or faked, can be a powerful management tool. If people think they can change your mind by making good arguments, they might try. You don't have time for that. It's much better to convince your employees that your brain is just *barely* able to keep your internal organs working. That's the optimal weasel zone. Take a lesson from this boss:

Dear Mr. Adams,

At a former job, my department got a 15 percent increase in our wage budget to pay for long-overdue raises. We were ecstatic at the news.

But when I got my job review, my smiling boss awarded me a 2 percent raise. When I asked why I wasn't getting the full 15 percent raise, he looked shocked and said that it had to be divided between the other ten people in the department, and that I was lucky to get 2 percent instead of 1 percent, like most people.

Incredulous, I pointed out that since the entire wage budget went up 15 percent, then every employee could, in theory, get a 15 percent raise. He burst out laughing, since it was apparently the most ridiculous concept he'd ever heard. I didn't get a penny more.

Management Entertainment

Most of your random policies are designed to at least look as if they're good for the company. But sometimes you'll be in the mood to yank the chains of your employees and you don't care who knows. Here are two of the most creative methods I've seen.

From the e-mail bag:

> Dear Mr. Adams,
>
> Our VP of HR decided that we needed to boost morale and started a "New Attitude" campaign. She's not interested in discovering WHY we aren't happy. Her idea was to fine anyone who was not smiling $1 per infraction. Now we're disgruntled AND poor!

> Dear Mr. Adams,
>
> It's gotten weird around here. The managers disappeared to some training for three days. Now they are being nice. Everyone is really creeped-out, and we are trying to figure out what it means. I think more layoffs. I think they went to a course that told them if they were nice, cutting staff would be perceived as nice.
>
> It's possible that the purpose was sincere, but the trainer obviously did not understand that us little people don't really care if they are nice or not.
>
> They are viewed as weasels because they are weasels, and not just because they act like weasels. Now we just

have thespian weasels, which is just as bad and much more annoying and distracting.

My bet is that it will last until Halloween, at which point they will transmogrify into something else. Views in the office range from one week to three months.

Let me know if you have seen this sort of thing and if you know of any effective defensive. Do you think garlic would work?

Nonthreatening Employees

If you make the mistake of hiring competent employees and training them, then your boss can someday replace you with one of your excellent employees. The safest balance as far as your career is concerned is to hire people who *look* competent (no dopey faces) but can barely find their way home.

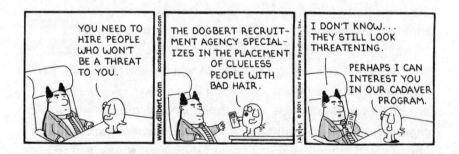

Dysfunctional employees have another benefit too. They're like ammo for the weasel manager. You can launch them at proj-

ects that are managed by your rivals within the company. You
might even be perceived as being helpful.

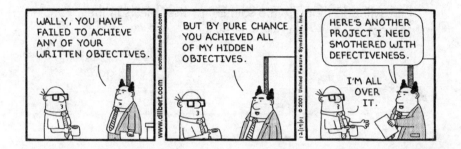

Weasel Trap

If you are a weasel manager and you have no idea what your
employees do all day, you'll need to invent some imagined
defects so you have something to criticize them about. Otherwise
it won't look as if you're managing. Your weasel employees
won't want to admit their own faults so you'll have to trick them
into it by setting a weasel trap. It works like this: Just ask them
what they are *good* at. Then twist it around so it sounds bad.

Any positive trait can be weasel-worded to sound like a flaw.
For example, if you are *accurate,* then you are too much of a *perfectionist.* If you are the sort of person who always *sees the big picture,* then you don't have good *attention to details.* If you *work
long hours,* that's the same as *not knowing how to manage your
time.* If you *don't ask inane questions* during meetings, you're *not
participating.* If you *do your important work* instead of being
diverted down rabbit trails by disorganized coworkers, then you're
not a team player. If you're *smart,* you're *too analytical.*

See how easy this is?

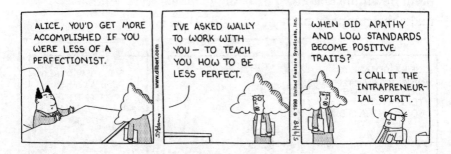

Weasel Communication

The goal of weasel communication is to say as much as possible without saying anything. One popular method used by executives during difficult times is to have a "town hall" type of meeting with employees. That's a large gathering where the employees are invited to write down their questions on three-by-five cards and submit them to the executives ahead of time. The questions might look like these:

Town Hall Meeting Questions

Eat my socks, you bald SOB! I want my 401K money back!

After you downsize me, can I have a job waxing your collection of antique roadsters?

Please settle a bet for us. What do you call the wife that comes after the trophy wife?

A meeting organizer will sort through the questions and edit them down to something like "How can we work without pay to make the company more successful?"

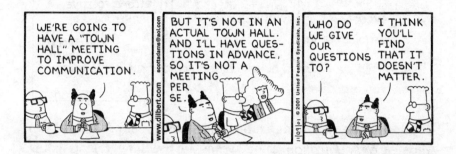

Weasel communication is popular in other fields too, from politics to parenting to romance. It's important to protect the ones you love from the truth, especially if you're afraid of what they might do to you when they find out. It's also important to keep the truth from your enemies. By process of elimination, that leaves a thin layer of people in the general population who don't care whether you live or die. You can tell those people the unweaseled truth without much risk. But you'll have to run after them and shout it because they're not interested.

Weasel Retirement

Weasel retirement is the sort of retirement where you keep your job and your paycheck but not the actual work. It is a rare and much-sought-after situation, and it can be yours if you play your cards right.

If you are a manager and would like to receive your manager-level pay without doing any managing, combine these two time-honored weasel techniques:

1. Announce that from now on you will "manage by exception," meaning that you will only get involved in problem areas.

2. Train your staff to believe that it's career suicide to bring you a problem.

Once your staff understands that they shouldn't talk to you about anything that is going wrong or anything that is going right, you have achieved weasel retirement.

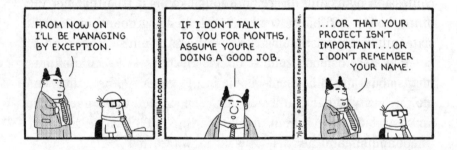

Another cushy job is chairman of the board. As far as I can tell, the company president is the one who runs the company. The CEO's job is bossing around the president. That's easier than running the company, but still work. However, the chairman enjoys full weasel retirement. As you work your way up the chain of management, you tend to know less and less about the specifics of a wider and wider scope of activities in the company until eventually you know absolutely nothing about everything. Then you become chairman, which, as the name implies, involves sitting in a chair.

Withholding Information

As a weasel boss, you want your employees to believe you have no useful information whatsoever. If they suspect that you know anything important, they'll spend all their free time trying to get it out of you. Try to establish a reputation as being the "last to know." After a reorganization or layoff is announced company-wide, make a show of saying, "What? No one mentioned that to me! I must be out of the loop."

Sometimes your weasel employees will try to trap you into a confession by asking direct questions like "Is it true that the VP of marketing will be moved to a 'special assignment' on March sixteenth as a punishment for being incompetent?"

Your best defense against direct questions is to make statements about the universe itself, such as "I guess anything is possible" or "I can't see the future." Those responses sound like answers and buy you time to scurry into your office until it all blows over.

Communicating with your employees is like being a frightened chunk of marble in a room full of sculptors. They'll try to chip away at everything you say until by process of elimination they figure out the truth. For example, if they're trying to find out if you're planning to bail out of the company and go to a new job, they'll go at it indirectly. They might ask you to schedule a 360-degree feedback session to give you input about your job performance. They know that if you agree to a meeting that involves employees telling you that you're an incompetent dolt, you're obviously planning to leave the company before that day.

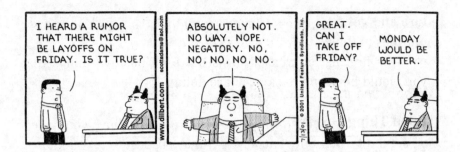

Talking Like a Business Weasel

If you want to be a respected business weasel, you must learn to speak incomprehensibly on a wide range of topics. Avoid saying anything useful because that sort of thing can come back and bite you.

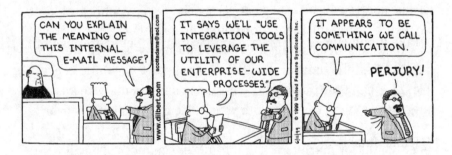

A good way to start being incomprehensible is by memorizing the handy phrases below and liberally sprinkling them into your conversations. They can be used in any order and about any subject where you want to show that you have a command of the situation. If you need a lead-in for your nonsense sentences, use the handy phrase "At the end of the day . . ."

Example: "At the end of the day we have to see the big picture and get back to basics, line up the ducks, touch bases, dip our toes in the water, and swing for the fence."

This first list of weasel phrases are all positive things that you would be proud to say you are doing.

Good Things to Be Doing

See the big picture	Line up the ducks	Have a sidebar
Get on the same page	Move goal posts	Put it on the back/front burner
Touch base	Dip our toes in the water	Table it for later
Get a handle on it	Build a straw man	Get more bang for your buck
Take it and run with it	Make a no-brainer decision	Set aggressive but achievable goals
Keep ahead of the game	Shorten launch curves	Manage from the top down
Think outside of the box	Embrace change	Manage expectations
Swing for the fence	Do a sanity check	Take a temperature check
View it from thirty thousand feet	Get buy-in	Press the flesh
Get back to basics	Put it to bed	Reach out

See what's coming down the pike	Take a rain check	Throw that dead cat in someone else's backyard
Make sure the left hand knows what the right hand is doing	Stretch the envelope	Run it up a flagpole and see who salutes
Sing from the same hymn sheet	Peel the onion	
Hit the ground running	Drill down into the data	

This next list includes things you want to avoid saying you're doing. They work best as descriptions of other people's work.

Things You Don't Want to Do

Reinvent the wheel	Find yourself on a slippery slope	Miss the window of opportunity
Raise a red flag	Shuffle the deck chairs	Have scope creep
Jump on the grenade	Make a career-limiting move	Have feature creep
Fall on the sword	Get lost in the noise	

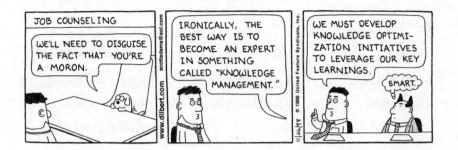

A good all-purpose phrase that you can interject in almost any business conversation is "This is not rocket science." The other weasels will nod and agree, none wanting to seem like the only weasel who thinks the topic at hand might be challenging.

Another good utility phrase is "I use the eighty/twenty rule." Toss it into the conversation at any time. This will generate strong agreement because it fits any situation where you have no data. It doesn't even matter what part is the eighty and what is the twenty. It just always sounds right.

For example, if you're waiting for people to arrive for a meeting you could say, "For any business meeting, eighty percent of the people come on time and twenty percent are late." That sounds totally reasonable. But if you say it the other way around, it sounds just as reasonable: "For any business meeting, twenty percent of the people come on time and the other eighty percent are late." It's like magic.

You can disguise almost any level of ignorance via the clever use of weasel vocabulary. The next time you're applying for a job, try memorizing the words on this list and using them in alphabetical order the way they are shown here. I guarantee that by the time you get to the *m* section you will have a job offer.

Business Weasel Words

accountable	capability	core competencies
action item	cash cow	cost-effective
alignment	caveat emptor	cost-reduction
applications	challenge	cross-fertilization
architecture	change agents	cross-functional teamwork
ballpark	change management	customer-focused
bells and whistles	channels	day-to-day
benchmark	cherry-picking	deliverables
best practice	client-centric	delta
bottom line	collaboration	deployments
brand	compatible	desktop environment
brand equity	compensation plan	develop
bread and butter	competitive advantage	digital
breakthrough products	consumer-driven	discipline
B2B	contingencies	disconnects
business case	continuous improvement	disengaged
business units	contribution	distribution channels

documentation

dotcom

e-business

efficiencies

empower

enterprise

e-services

e-tailers

eyeballs

facilitates

faster

fast track

flow charts

focus

focus groups

framework

functional

game plan

gap analysis

goal-directed

goals

guesstimate

hardball

hardware

high level

human capital

identified

implementation

incentivize

incremental

information

initiatives

innovative

inside-out
organization

integrated

interactive

interface

internal and
external functions

intranet

key performance
indicator

key strategic areas

leadership

lean manufacturing

lessons learned

leveraging

line operation

living document

long term

management
consultant

maximizing

metrics

milestones

mission-critical

mission statement

mobile

movers and
shakers

next steps

objectives

off-line

operationalize

opportunity

outsourcing

paradigms

paradigm shift

parallel

partner

performance

positioning

proactive

process

product

profitability

quality

quantifiable benefit

real-time basis

reciprocal

red tape

requirements

reseller

resource

responsive

results-driven

revisit

rightsizing

risk management

robust

service

shareholder value

showstoppers

software

solutions

specifications

standardization

step change

strategic fit

suboptimal

synergies

teamwork

technology
platforms

thought leadership

tools

track record

traction

transaction flow

transforming

turnkey

unquantifiable
benefit

utilizing

value-added

values

viral

vision

warm and fuzzy

war stories

whole nine yards

win-win

world-class

Examples of weasel words abound. As I was writing this section of the book, I got an e-mail from my comic syndicator, United Media, giving me the good news that they had signed an important deal to host something called "interstitials" on the dilbert.com Web site. For this we would receive money. Woo-hoo! We'd been getting a lot of complaints about pop-up ads on the Web site—those annoying ads that cover the page you want to view—so I was delighted that we would be using interstitials instead, whatever those were. Lately advertisers wouldn't pay for anything but pop-up ads, and I had been lobbying for a more creative solution. I had high hopes for these new things called interstitials.

You're probably way ahead of me on this. It turns out that *interstitials* is another word for pop-up ads.

I'm glad I live in a world that has no problems—only issues, challenges, and opportunities. That's why I hardly ever consider proactively reorganizing my soul to a new opportunity in the afterlife.

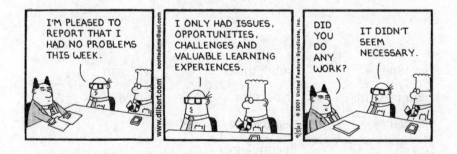

From my e-mail bag:

Dear Mr. Adams,

I just heard a new one. The company proclaims it is now experiencing "accelerated refreshment of the organization." In other words, it is firing lots of people and doing it fast.

Dear Mr. Adams,

My company (a large technical corporation) has been forced to cut back the workforce. There were layoffs in June, and many people feared more cuts, especially at the end of the quarter. The president of the company, to boost morale, sent out a letter claiming that there would be no layoffs, only "performance-based departures." We're not being downsized, fired, cut back, laid off, or right-sized. We're experiencing performance-based departures.

Dear Mr. Adams,

This is an actual requirement listed for a marketing job on a job-posting Web site:
    "Proven ability to deal with ambiguity in a rapidly changing environment."
    Why not just say, "Ability to curb homicidal tendencies despite asinine leadership"?

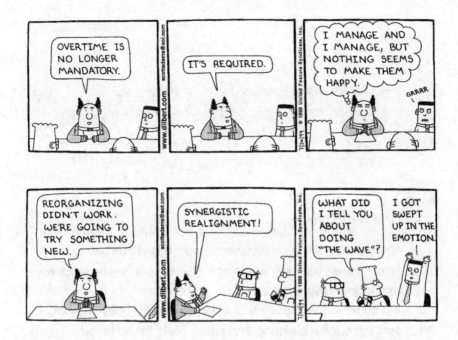

Dear Mr. Adams,

Here at [oil company] in Saudi Arabia, they actually have an undertaker on staff, though he is not named on the company payroll as such. His official title is "personnel adviser."

Weasel words are not limited to the workplace. Here's an excellent example of weasel words in the romance department.

Dear Mr. Adams,

This is my most utterly weaseliest tale:
    An ex-boyfriend once said to me, "When I said I
wanted a permanent relationship, I didn't necessarily mean
with you."

Nepotism

As a weasel boss, you know that the most qualified person in the
world for any job whatsoever is yourself. But if you're not available, or the job requires actual work, you'll have to settle for second best: a close relative.

A relative shares some of the wonderful DNA that is coursing
through your bloodstream and clotting your brain. Your relative
might even look a little bit like you, and that's a bonus too.
There's no good reason to be looking at other people when you
can be looking at things that look like you.

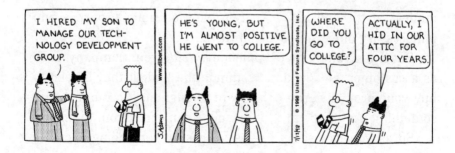

Budgets

A budget is a business tool for ensuring that managers buy
things they don't need. Most of that excess buying happens
toward the end of the year when managers realize they have
some budget money left over and they'll lose it if they don't use
it. That's free money. No one says no to free money.

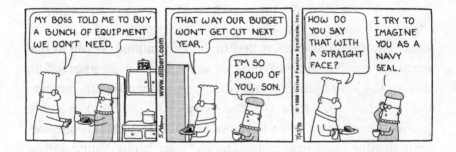

If you're talking to people inside your own company, you'll
want to pad your budget estimates and make everything seem as
if it costs more than it does. That way you'll have something to
"sacrifice" if budget cuts are announced. Or you'll have "free
money" at the end of the year to blow on holiday parties and
unnecessary office supplies and travel.

But if you're talking to someone *outside* your company, such
as a customer, always underestimate the budget they'll need to
buy your products. You don't want to frighten a customer with
something like the truth. Nothing good can come from that.

So as you can see, there is no case where being accurate
about budgets is a good thing. The only tricky part is remember-
ing when to inflate them and when to underestimate them.

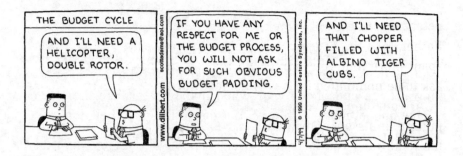

The biggest threat to your budget happiness is "preliminary numbers." Your senior management might ask you for preliminary budget numbers for an important meeting. They might even tell you that the preliminary numbers can change later and that's okay. Don't fall for that trick. As soon as a senior management person hears a number, it gets stuck in his skull like a ship in a bottle. Any number he hears after that point will be considered wrong. From that point forward your performance will be judged against the preliminary numbers.

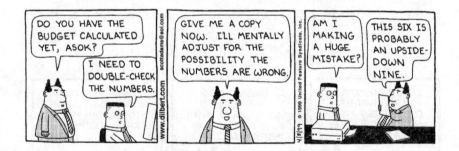

Later in the year you can try to convince your boss that you went over your budget because the *budget itself* was wrong and not because you're incompetent. But you want to word that argument carefully. It's never persuasive to say, "I am not incom-

petent regardless of how many facts seem to suggest otherwise."
Rather, take the positive side and point out that you could have
spent more, but you didn't, and that's a savings of sorts. Then
ask to be nominated for a role model award.

If your upper management is micromanaging your budget,
putting limits on individual line items instead of just watching
the total, then you need the weasel's ultimate weapon: creative
classification.

Creative classification: The theory that a rhinoceros is exactly
the same as a chipmunk with a big nose.

Let's say that you're out of money for hiring temps but you
still have money in the furniture budget. And you don't need any
furniture but you do need some temp help. The nonweasel
would be stymied by this situation. But the weasel has an obvious solution: hire some temps and classify them as furniture.
This might require the temps to wear oak varnish instead of
clothing, and to kneel in corners with lamps on their heads, but
you're beating the system and that's what counts.

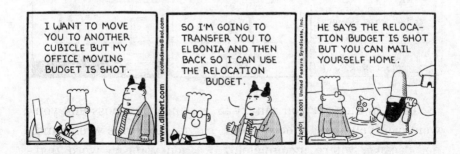

Getting Input

It's always a good idea to gather lots of opinions from your staff before making important decisions. That way, when you do whatever you were planning to do anyway, you'll look like a person who cares about the opinions of other people, not like the manipulative, autocratic weasel that you are.

Never make the mistake of asking only one person for an opinion. That's the worst possible situation. When you ask one person for advice, then ignore it, you are sending this subtle message:

> I only wanted to hear your opinion so I could get together
> with friends later and laugh at you behind your back. Based
> on your opinion, and the shape of your skull, I have a theory
> that you are the missing link between apes and people.

Taking advice would be okay if "other people" had wisdom. But in my experience, getting wisdom from "other people" is like milking a bull: it looks as if it might work, but you'll be disappointed in the result.

In fact—and at the risk of belaboring this point—if you had some valuable wisdom and you wanted to hide it where no one would ever think of looking, I would recommend giving it to "other people."

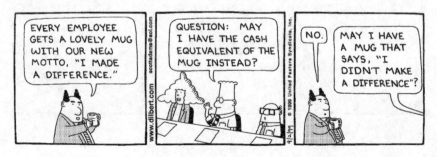

Employee References

If you are a boss, sooner or later a bad employee will ask you for a job reference. This is one of the purest weasel choices in the world: a chance to transfer your problem to someone you don't even know. It doesn't get any better than that.

The secret to writing a reference letter is to focus on what the employee did right while downplaying any problem areas. For example, if the employee ignored safety procedures and caused a toxic fire that forced the evacuation of a town and the permanent closing of a factory, you could say he reduced payroll expenses. If he stole from coworkers, you could say he found creative sources of financing. If he organized the accounting department into a satanic cult, you could say he's a team-builder.

Never give a bad employee a bad reference. If you do, only three things can happen, and none of them are good:

1. The employee sues you.

2. The employee uses you as human sacrifice in his satanic cult.

3. The employee continues working for you.

7

Negotiating Like a Weasel

Negotiate is a word that was invented by businesspeople so they could talk about their work without using synonyms for copulation.

Wife:	How was work today, dear?
Husband:	Great! I had the customer by the ears and I was negotiating the heck out of him!
Daughter:	Mommy, what does *negotiate* mean?
Wife:	Um . . . it's what two people do when they love each other.
Husband:	*Ha ha!* I was slapping his butt and yelling, *"Who's your vendor?! Who's your vendor?!"*

Weasel Misquote

When you're planning to buy anything expensive, you probably call around to compare prices. Companies have wised up to that strategy and counter it with the weasel tactic known as the accidental misquote. You'll get something closer to the real price when they know you're done shopping around. But if you smell like a looky-loo, you always get the accidental weasel misquote. Here are a few true examples from the past week.

I called a hotel to ask for prices. A few hours later I called again to make the reservation. The price was $100 higher. The reservation person said she was sure she had told me the right price the first time.

While planning another trip a few days later, I called another hotel and asked about prices. I made a reservation and happily went about my business. A few hours later the hotel reservation clerk called me to tell me he had "looked at the wrong price sheet" and the real price was $100 higher.

A vendor told me that his price would include absolutely everything needed for the project, from nuts to bolts, from A to Z. He went out of his way to emphasize how comprehensive the budget was. It was a matter of great pride. Just for laughs I listed about ten large expenses that I thought weren't included in his budget. He confessed that none of those items are included in the phrase "everything is included."

The trusting part of me (a tiny little vestigial organ somewhere deep in my body now covered with bile) wants to believe that all of those misquotes were genuine accidents. But I can't escape this nagging question:

Question: Why are there no accidental misquotes in the too high direction?

Answer: Weasels.

Leaving Things Out

When you give someone a price quote, leave out as many costs as possible. That will make the price seem too low to resist. Most customers will forget to ask about things like taxes, installation, delivery permit fees, insurance, warranty extensions, service contracts, cables, and whatnot. A skilled weasel can convince the average ignorant consumer that a $1,000 item actually sells for 5¢. Once the consumer is psychologically committed to making the deal, and the final paperwork is produced, the sales weasel totals up the "extras."

Phone companies are the experts in this technique. According to my phone bill, I'm only paying about $2 a month for actual phone service but another $100 for all the costs that the evil government forces them to pass through to me. I'm subsidizing deaf people, hillbillies, and the elderly. I'm even paying a special tax for the state regulators who are responsible for this mess, i.e., I am paying a special tax to pay people to confuse me. I'm definitely getting my money's worth.

Seriously, I counted ten lines of various "Taxes & Surcharges" on my local phone bill. One is something called the "California High Cost Fund Surcharge." I think that means I'm being taxed for the right to be overcharged.

Claim That You Are Losing Money

If you negotiate with a weasel, sooner or later he will tell you he is losing money on your deal. Here's a good way to handle that.

> ***Weasel:*** I'm losing money on this deal.
>
> ***You:*** So, are you saying that you're a moron?
>
> ***Weasel:*** What? No! I'm just choosing to lose money on this deal because I'm nice.

> **You:** Let me get this straight. You're selling things below your own costs, and you know it, yet you choose to continue doing it?
>
> **Weasel:** That's right. Because that's the kind of guy I am.
>
> **You:** The moron kind?

The Price Depends

Here's something that you, the savvy consumer, should never do: tell a repairman how much you think something will cost before you get the estimate. I made that mistake recently.

A large piece of equipment in my house was malfunctioning. I asked my service guy what it would cost to replace it. He shrugged and said he didn't have a guess off the top of his head, despite that this was his business. Thinking I could cleverly pin him down to a range, I tossed out a number. "Is it under ten thousand dollars?" I asked.

He got a stunned look on his face and hesitated before answering, "Yes . . . it's definitely under ten thousand dollars." He offered to fax me a quote in a few days. I think he was skipping when he left. When the fax came in, the quote was $9,900 and was notable for its lack of detail. Normally I'm too lazy to get multiple quotes for anything. But this price struck me as a bit coincidental, and this particular equipment could be priced on the Internet in about two minutes. It turns out that the equipment retails for about $1,500.

I found a new service guy.

Did you ever have a car salesman ask you, "How much were you planning to spend?" That's how sales professionals determine in the first five seconds whether you're a complete idiot.

Wrong answer:　　I have $16,000 in my bank account but I can charge another $2,000 on my Visa and borrow $700 from my mother.

Right answer:　　I was *planning* to spend $5, you stinkin' weasel.

From my e-mail:

Dear Mr. Adams,

I used to sell cars. Being a nineteen-year-old female, I got a lot of crap from my fellow all-male staff plus the customers that have chips on their shoulders for obvious reasons.

One day, a thirty-something guy came in with his two boys, who were about six and seven years old. He must have wanted to show them what a big man he was, so when I walked up to him, he looked at me and said he wanted to speak to a salesman. I told him politely that I was a salesperson and would be happy to help him. After about twenty seconds of him looking me up and down he said, "Honey, you just a little girl. You can't know nothing 'bout automobiles!"

I told him that I would do the best I could and asked him several questions about what he was looking for. The last question was how much he was planning to spend. "Oh, a lot," he said, "about fourteen thousand dollars." He finished, "A dumb-looking girl like you probably don't make enough to buy the cars you sell."

I said, "I have the perfect car for you, sir." I showed him the four-door Geo Metro he was standing right next to. I also mentioned that it was on sale for $13,995. We drove it and he loved it. When I was taking the info off the car to write up the numbers, I conveniently took out the price sticker that said MSRP was $11,500 (with dealer markup). He paid the full price of $13,995.

Wear Down the Other Side

If you're an unpleasant middle-aged guy, sometimes you can wear down a negotiating opponent by being affable. Nothing is quite as unpleasant as an affable middle-aged guy who won't stop talking for hours on end. And you can't yell at someone for being affable, so it's a powerful technique.

Obviously this technique doesn't work when your opponent is female. Women are energized by blather. They feed off it. It actually makes them stronger. Women even have a word for it— *conversation.*

After your opponent thinks the negotiations are finished and is mentally and emotionally drained, toss in a few extras and act as if you had forgotten them. Continue to be affable. Say you'd be glad to reopen the entire negotiation if "you think that's absolutely necessary."

Insane Forgetting

I used to negotiate with a weasel who was notorious for "forgetting" his end of any agreement no matter how many times it had been discussed and agreed, even in writing. Later, when I protested, he would begin negotiations anew and insist that whatever I had already done for my part of the agreement wasn't relevant to the discussion because it was in the past and you can't change the past.

This is like the old joke about the lawyer who argues that the court should have mercy on a client who killed his parents because he's an orphan. The weird thing is that the method works, because once you realize you're dealing with a psycho, you're quite happy with anything you can get in return because it could be worse.

The insane-forgetting weasel technique can be used over and over again on the same victim. That's the great thing about insanity: there's no wrong time to use it.

Wait Until You're at the Deadline

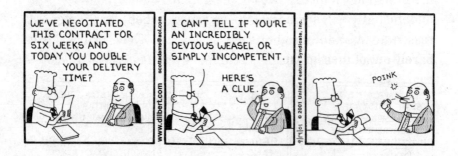

In every negotiation, one side will get more hosed than the other side if an impending deadline is missed. If your opponent has the most to lose, let the deadline get as near as possible before doing your serious negotiating.

For example, if you're a heart transplant surgeon, negotiate your price after you have the donated heart in your hand and your customer has turned a deep purple. Go out to the waiting room and ask the family members if they want to pay extra for you to use a surgical mask or would they prefer to take the chance you'll sneeze into the open chest cavity.

Use Weaseleze

Weaseleze is the official tongue of weasels. It's composed of words that make perfect sense individually, but when artfully arranged, they become misleading or impenetrable.

Weaseleze is used often in advertising, legal work, employee performance reviews, and dating. When used in a legal contract, the goal is to make the wording just *barely* incomprehensible. If you go too far, the other side will complain and you'll have to change it. But if you construct the weaseleze in a way that makes the other side think, "If only I were a *little* bit smarter, I would understand," that's a home run. Most people will be too embarrassed to admit they don't understand something if it seems just barely out of their grasp.

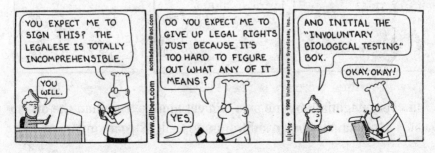

Sometimes the length of a contract alone will be enough to discourage the other side from reading it. Most deals can be described on one page, but thanks to the miracle of weaseleze most contracts can be stretched to thirty or forty pages of mind-numbing trivia. If you slap down a contract in front of someone and hand him a pen, there will be added pressure to sign without reading. No one wants to look befuddled. That's the sort of label that can stay with you.

Sometimes when I know I'm going to sign a weighty document without reading it, I'll flip through the pages as if I'm speed-reading. Then I'll quickly point to some obscure section or word and ask for clarification, as if that is the one thing that I don't immediately understand. I try to leave the impression that I'm some sort of fast-reading genius. Feel free to borrow that technique.

Be Specific

A well-written contract is very specific. The more specific it is, the less you give away. If you're clever enough, you can actually be so specific that you don't commit to give anyone anything.

Dear Mr. Adams,

I just had a house built. The contract included a completion clause making the building company pay if the house wasn't finished by the date promised.

Unfortunately for us, the terminology of the clause is such that it only gets invoked if they can't "provide access" to the house. So on the promised date they provided access: they gave us a key. Voilà! Never mind that there's nowhere to bathe. (We've been visiting our gym daily for the last month for showering.)

Specificity isn't just for written contracts. It's handy for any sort of commitment, as in this example:

Dear Mr. Adams,

I work in the communications industry as a project manager. I received this quote from a database administrator when he was moving software into production: "Don't say the automated feed will work. That is too strong. We need to weasel it. Say the infrastructure is in place to *allow* it to work."

Go Out of Business

If your business offers warranties on your product or service, it's a good idea to go out of business occasionally. Roofing companies use this method with great success. They replace a few roofs and then go out of business before the rainy season. If you plan to go out of business, be sure to offer a lifetime warranty in your contract. That will give you a competitive advantage over the people who only offer twenty-year contracts and go out of business the same time you do.

Provide the Contract

Be the first one to draw up a first draft of the contract. Toss in lots of ridiculous clauses so you have plenty to negotiate away later.

Every inhabitant of earth can see this weasel trick coming a mile away and yet it still works. Our brains are wired to compare things, so if you first see something that's spectacularly odious, anything after that will seem pretty good in comparison. A good first offer for any contract should read roughly like this:

> You will give me huge piles of money while I kick your dog, set your house on fire, and make sweet, sweet love to your spouse. The parties agree to arbitration by armed intruders. This contract may be arbitrarily and secretly added to by one party (us) anytime we are feeling greedy and/or evil.

Make sure you pad the force majeure paragraph as much as possible. That's where you list examples of big catastrophes that are beyond human control. If a force majeure flattens your town, you don't have to live up to your end of the deal. (Sweet!) Make sure your force majeure list has more than the usual boring stuff like earthquakes, hurricanes, and floods. Add as many acts of god as you can think of:

1. An animal gets stuck inside your wall and dies.

2. You become allergic to color.

3. God decides to make an example out of you.

Thanks to the use of e-mail and digital files, contracts are like fungus, growing new paragraphs and sprouting new words from the beginning of negotiations to the end. It's considered sporting to flag any changes to the contract before you send it to the other party, but my experience has been that sometimes the other people "forget" or sometimes, halfway through the process, they accidentally include language from entirely different contracts. Sometimes they even revert to earlier versions and "lose" language that has already been negotiated and agreed. None of these things are crimes, oddly enough. So you should take advantage of this method as much as possible. It's free, sometimes effective, and you can always claim incompetence as your alibi.

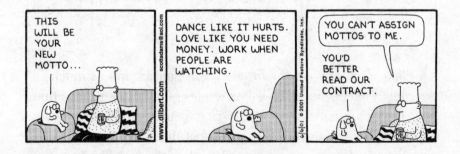

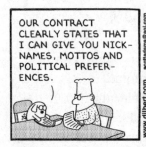
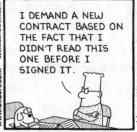
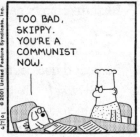

Extra Services

Most people are optimists (another word for dumb) and don't expect problems when they start a project. Smart weasel vendors will negotiate contracts that are reasonable if everything goes according to plan. Later, when the project becomes a raging disaster—as all projects do—the clever weasel makes a killing by charging an hourly rate to fix all the problems.

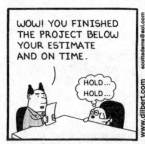
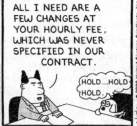
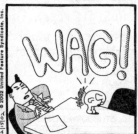

In the unlikely event that problems don't happen naturally, the weasel can create some problems and then charge the customer to fix them. Most customers will complain, so your best bet is to blame the victim for your mistake.

Example:

> **Customer:** Hey, you installed my air-conditioning system in the middle of my living room!!!
>
> **Weasel:** If that's a problem I can relocate it, but it'll cost you $100 per hour and I don't know how long it will take.
>
> **Customer:** What?! But it's *your* fault!
>
> **Weasel:** You never specified where it should go. I can't be paying for your lack of clarity!

Big, Dumb, Stubborn People

Big, dumb people can sometimes get their way simply by being stubborn. Big, dumb, *and* stubborn is a potent combination, one that I call the tridefecta. When you deal with someone who is blessed with the tridefecta, you know it's easier to give in than to fight. I think I speak for all smallish people when I say that big people are scary. They take up too much room, and when they perspire, they make a high-pitched sound that is only audible to people under five feet nine.

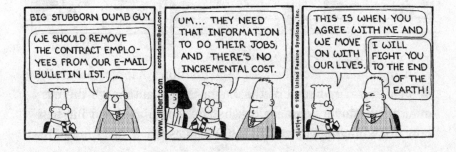

Inventing Numbers

Weasels know that our brains are wired in a way that makes anything with numbers—even inaccurate numbers—more persuasive than anything without numbers. For example, evaluate the persuasiveness of these two statements:

1. If you lend me a million dollars, I'll give it back later with a little extra.

2. If you lend me a million dollars, you will earn $3,246,946.38 in 2.3 years.

The second statement is far more persuasive. Someone obviously did some research. The average person will look at it and think, "Even if it took as long as two and a half years, it would still be a good deal."

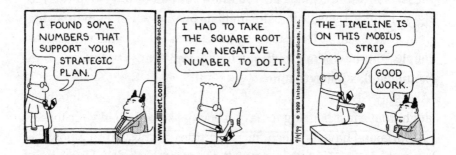

The Kevin Bacon Gambit

You've probably heard of the Kevin Bacon game, where everyone in the movie business can be connected to Kevin Bacon by only a few degrees of separation. Weasels use a variation of that game to make strangers do their bidding. This method has been used on me hundreds of times, so I can attest to its power.

It works like this: If you're normal, you have a small circle of friends, family, and business contacts that you simply "can't say no" to. So if a complete stranger needs a favor from you, he will start sniffing around until he finds a string of connections from himself to you. But it needs to be a special kind of connection where everyone in the chain can't say no to the person upstream until it gets all the way to you. The next thing you know, your neighbor—who could rat you out to the homeowners' association about your illegal gazebo—is asking you to donate money to a charity for flatulent pug dogs. Your neighbor doesn't want to ask you, but he's an insurance broker and his biggest customer asked him to ask you. And so on, up the chain of connections until you realize you're being controlled by a nine-year-old boy in Paraguay.

Important Titles

People who have important jobs don't need impressive titles. For example, if a surgeon wanted to put on his business card "Almighty Giver of Life" or "Exalted Savior," no patient is going to laugh; that's just begging to have a sponge sewed up in your torso.

Surgeons have no need for fancy titles. But if you're a powerless cubicle worker who is trying to negotiate with a customer, it's a good idea to have an inflated title with *vice president* in the name. That's a big advantage. It's hard for your undertitled opponent to say no to a vice president, especially if his own title is something like Assistant Pimple on the Company's Left Buttock.

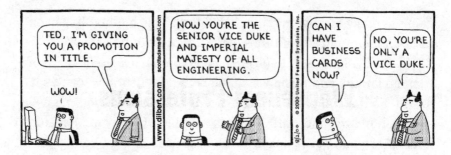

Meeting Weight

Every person possesses an invisible yet tangible meeting weight. Your meeting weight is a measure of how much the other people will listen to your opinions and how much they fear you. You never want to attend a meeting when the "other side" has more weight. That's why it's often necessary to bring with you a group of unnecessary tagalongs to tip the balance your way.

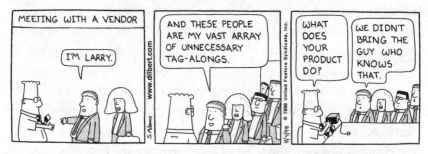

The tagalongs, also known as meeting dingleberries, are especially important if you are going to see a client. Clients automatically have more meeting weight than vendors because clients have the money. So the smart vendor will load the meeting with dingleberries. A good strategy is to select one feeble and pathetic-looking dingleberry who, by his appearance, suggests he will be the first one fired if the client doesn't buy your service. If he can get moist-eyed on demand, that's a plus.

8

Weaseliest Professions

If I didn't already have an easy job, I would want to be an archaeologist. I think I could be the most famous archaeologist who ever lived. If I found a toenail in the desert—even if it was my own—I would construct an elaborate theory of the primitive society that once lived there, complete with full-scale models of the mighty beasts that roamed the plains.

In fact, I'd be great at any profession where it's hard to verify whether you are a maverick visionary or a stinkin' weasel. For example, I think I could be a famous physicist, as long as I stuck to theory and didn't try to detonate any bombs. I'd fill my whiteboard with equations that were "in progress" and pile lots of technical journals on my desk and floor and then stare at my computer for hours. Every few months I would write a paper full of things that were so smart-sounding that my readers would be forced to assume the confusion was originating in their own brains. Like this:

The gray hole has gravitational pull so massive that it bends light into an adjacent dimension and back again thus causing tiny strings to vibrate into an elongated funnel of time.

Then I'd say, "If that doesn't make sense, maybe you should have paid more attention in school."

I would also like to be a defense lawyer for guilty murderers in a state that has capital punishment. That way I could feel pretty good about myself no matter which way things go. If I win and put a killer back on the street, I'm an excellent lawyer! If I lose, a murderer gets fried, and that's not a bad day's work either.

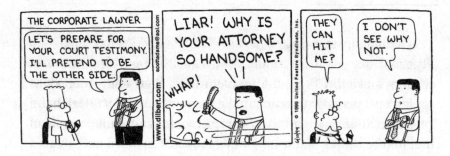

I wouldn't mind working for an ad agency either. In creative jobs there's no right answer. If you get good results with one out of three random tries, you'll be hailed as a genius. Then you can move to management and hire weasels to do the wild guessing for you.

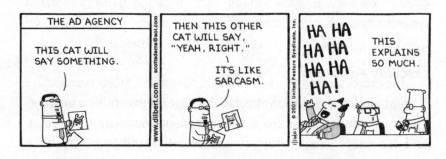

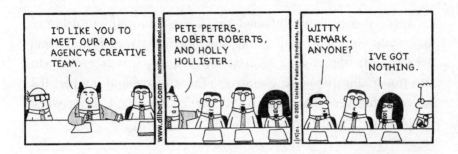

Cartooning is one of the best weasel jobs around. On a bad day I'll grunt out some horrible piece of three-panel confusion and readers inevitably think the problem is on their end. After all, it couldn't get printed if it didn't make any sense, could it? (Heh heh.) I try to include enough buzzwords to create reasonable suspicion that maybe there's some sort of inside joke. I'm aided and abetted by the millions of weasel readers who are only too happy to tell their coworkers, "That's the funniest Dilbert comic of all time. Only a moron wouldn't get it." (Thank you for the help.)

I would be bad at any sort of job that didn't have much margin for error—the kind where if I screwed up, someone would notice. For example, I would be a bad engineer for the space shuttle. I'd be all, "Can someone remind me if there's air in space, because I'm assuming there is."

Executive Assistants

A great job for a sadistic yet playful weasel is executive assistant. It's fun to abuse executives because they generally deserve it. And it's easy because they're gullible. Executives rarely have contact with the truth, so they don't even know what it looks like. That means they'll believe anything. That spells fun.

Once you have established some trust with your executive boss, you can begin the brainwashing by removing him from contact with the rest of society. As gatekeeper, you can make sure he sees only people you want him to see. Once you become his sole source of information and human contact, it's time to fill his head with amusing nonsense, like this:

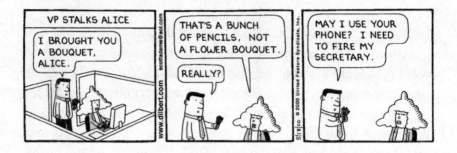

Writers

During my official cartoonist duties I've met about a jillion newspaper and magazine reporters. I've asked many of them why they chose their profession. The most common answer (I swear) is, "I'm lazy." They don't say, "And I'm a weasel," but I think that's implied.

As a writer myself (sort of), I sympathize. I too was attracted to this profession by the unbridled opportunity for leisure. I don't know what you did at your job today, but all I'm doing is sitting in a comfortable chair and moving my fingers. I'm wearing pajamas, sipping a diet Coke, and writing about myself. It doesn't get any better than this.

I start work at 5 A.M. every day. Sometimes I mention that fact while making a droopy face in an effort to garner sympathy.

But that's a weasel trick because I like waking up early. So I get the sympathy without the pain. It's good stuff.

I take some pride in beating the system, i.e., getting paid for the absolute least amount of effort. But just when I think I have achieved the pinnacle of weasel-ease, some other weasel tops me and I feel a burning urge to do even less work. I'm competitive that way.

I'm currently in a pitched weasel-fight with another writer who is trying to trick me into doing work for which he will get paid. He is about the millionth writer to try this same weasel maneuver with me, so I saw it coming from a mile away. This weasel technique goes like this. First the weasel identifies someone like me who is in the public eye but isn't important enough to have handlers or paid assassins to ward off weasels. Then the weasel asks for a short phone interview that I am happy to give. The weasel asks easy questions like "How old are you?" and "Where do you live?" He writes down the answers to these penetrating questions, thanks me, and goes away to write a fascinating story. Or so it seems.

Then he sends the e-mail follow-up questions that he "forgot" to ask. This is where the full beauty and magic of this weasel trick comes into play. The weasel saves his toughest essay questions for e-mail. These are open-ended questions for which I would have to write a feature-length article to make any sort of intelligent response. Here is a sample of the actual questions I got last night by e-mail:

After the Internet bubble, what is your assessment of this past technology cycle (through the letters you received and what you described in Dilbert)?

and . . .

> Since you began drawing Dilbert, what were the main
> changes you found in the corporate environment? Did this
> whole start-up boom transform how people think, work,
> manage downsizing and waste?

If I were to fall for this trick (which I have in the past), I would write a few pages of thoughtful answers and then e-mail it to the writer. Soon I would get a few more questions. By the end of this cycle I would have created an entire article that would be published under the writer's name as an interview with me. The so-called "writer" wouldn't even have to go through the trouble of typing because I'm doing that too.

You have to admit, it's brilliant. I haven't yet decided on my weasel countermeasure. I'll probably either lose his e-mail message or answer in one-sentence non sequiturs.

In Hollywood the laziest writers gravitate away from dramas that require research about icky medical procedures and complicated legal theories and toward situation comedies. The laziest among the comedy writers are all hoping for the ultimate prize: working on a sitcom about sitcom writers.

If you have any writing skills whatsoever, the hardest part of the job is coming up with new topics. I met a bunch of TV comedy writers during my stint doing the Dilbert TV show. Most of them were cleverly developing sitcom pilots about the lives of sitcom writers. The dream is that they could wake up in the morning with a craving for pancakes and then write a script about a comedy writer who wakes up in the morning with a craving for pancakes.

I suppose I can declare myself King of the Writing Weasels because I'm a writer who just wrote about people who write about themselves. This required little research. Excuse me while I take a sip of diet Coke.

Ahhh . . . that's tasty. Although I am feeling smug now, I know that eventually a book reviewer will write about how I wrote about people who write about themselves. And the crown will be passed.

If comedy and drama aren't your bag, and you still want to be a lazy writer, you can do what most action-movie writers do, i.e., practically nothing. Apparently there is only one action script in the world and it was written years ago. You know the one. It goes like this:

- A crime fighter doesn't "follow the rules."

- His boss gets mad at him for not following the rules.

- An evil bad guy makes the crime fighter mad, generally by killing or kidnapping a family member.

- The crime fighter's boss assigns a seemingly incompetent partner.

- Lots of things blow up, people get shot, cars crash.

- The crime fighter and the evil bad guy have a showdown in a large industrial complex that features steam coming out of various pipes and chains that hang from the ceiling.

- The crime fighter kills every member of the evil bad guy's gang, starting with the ones who had the least screen time.

- The crime fighter kills the evil bad guy's invincible assassin but gets beaten up and wounded in the process.

- The crime fighter kills the evil bad guy in a clever way using materials found in the large industrial complex (acid, wrecking ball, hot steam, power cables, etc.).

- The crime fighter falls in love with whoever insulted him the most during the so-called "plot."

- Everyone seems inexplicably happy despite hundreds of close friends, coworkers, and family members getting slain in the past hour.

All you need to do is change some of the names and details. For example, the large industrial complex could be extra-steamy. There is no limit to how creative the story can become.

Management-Book Writers

If reading a book on how to be successful could make you successful, then everyone would be a billionaire except illiterate people. And even they could become billionaires if they listened to the books on tape. What a great world that would be: the dumb managers would become smart and the lazy ones would become motivated just by reading management books. But in reality you hardly ever hear a manager say, "After reading this management book I realize I had always been a lazy, sadistic, clueless moron. But now I'm not!"

Despite their total lack of usefulness, business books are successful because there's a part of the human brain—called the stupidity lobe—that makes us believe that stories of successful people apply to our own situation. I've studied the stories of lots of successful people, and there's always a gap that looks like this:

- Worked as shoeshine boy

-

- Worked as busboy

-

- Worked as garbageman

-

- ***Unexplained gap in story***

-

- Bought a Manhattan landmark and turned it into a luxury hotel

The unexplained gap usually involves an inheritance, a marriage, or something illegal or lucky. The same is true of successful managers. There's always some point where they just happened to be in the right place at the right time, a situation usually referred to as being "a world-class manager" or alternatively, "lucky %#@*&!"

Statisticians rarely write management books because they know that a certain number of morons will succeed under any system by pure chance. Somewhere in the world there's a manager who rubs his head with a tongue depressor before every staff meeting and has experienced forty quarters of consecutive revenue growth. And right behind that manager is a management-book author taking notes and getting ready to write *The Tongue Depressor Management Method.*

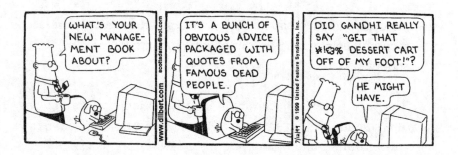

Safety Weasels

Sometimes large companies have safety departments. This is one of the greatest weasel jobs of all time because *safety* is an ambiguous weasel word that leaves plenty of wiggle room. Almost anything can kill you if you eat it, sit on it, trip over it, or set it on fire.

If you haven't done anything useful lately and it's time to give your accomplishments to your boss—no problem. Just look around your cubicle and find something that could kill a person under the right conditions. Then schedule a training class to teach people not to, for example, sit on pencils, lick electrical outlets, and light their own farts. The goal is that fewer people die from those causes after your class than before, and since you're the only one collecting the data, that's no problem.

Sometimes the inspiration for safety ideas finds you. If I were the safety director, I would sit in my office all day and wait for news that some employee had found a new way to kill himself with a common workplace item, such as a chair or a paper clip. Then I would send around e-mail "safety bulletins" explaining the proper use of said killer item. I might even make up some statistics, e.g.:

According to the National Bureau of Dangerous Items, three thousand employees per year die from premature binder snapping.

The way I see it, accuracy is strictly optional when you're writing something that no one will read. Later, when someone else dies from a binder-snapping wound, you can accuse him of not reading his safety bulletins. The more people that die, the more important your job seems to your boss. So you don't want to make things too safe and put yourself out of the best weasel job in the world.

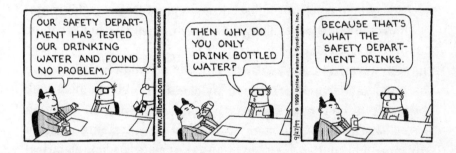

Suggestions of Threat

The best kinds of jobs are the ones where you don't need to threaten customers because they're already afraid of you. Good examples of those types of jobs are:

1. Drug kingpins

2. Police

3. Banks

I often get calls from people who claim to be police officers collecting money for suspicious-sounding charities. I'm afraid to say no. I worry that someday a burglar will be in my house, I'll call the police, and they'll run a check on my donation record before deciding whether to save my life or eat a doughnut. So I find myself in the ironic position of hoping that the person asking for money on the phone is a criminal posing as a police officer and not an actual police officer. Crooks are less of a threat because they don't keep good records. They won't know if I donated or not. But police have computers in their cars. A cop can enter my license plate number into the system and decide whether to wrestle a mugger off my back or just sit in the car and spray bullets in my general direction and hope for the best.

Banks are scary too. They take your money and put it somewhere you can't see it. I worry that if my bank gets mad at me, they can just make my money "go away." So when my bank tells me it will take five days to clear my check from the bank across the street, I don't make sarcastic comments about their computerized check-clearing system. I don't point out that thanks to advanced fiber optics a series of bits can travel across the street in well under five days even on a slow day. No, I smile and *thank them* for keeping my money for themselves for four days. Sometimes I even bid them good day.

Criminals

Obviously I am exaggerating when I say people are stinkin' weasels. There are exceptions, notably career criminals. You have to appreciate criminals because they care enough about the truth to always dress and act exactly like criminals. You never see a mug shot of a career criminal and think, "He looks so nice. I'm surprised to hear that he strangled forty people." Career criminals give you exactly what their packaging promises. As a repeat victim, I respect that.

Gang members take it one step further, using a sophisticated color-coded garment system so there's no ambiguity about what they do for a living. I've taken prescription drugs that have less information on the container.

The truth-in-labeling ethic of professional gang members is impressive. Say for example a gang member squeezes through your bathroom window at 3 A.M. and—because it's a tight fit and there's broken glass—he accidentally rips off all of his distinctive criminal clothing. Suddenly he's standing in your dining room, wearing nothing but sneakers. Your first reaction—because there are no color-coded gang garments to signal his intentions—might be to think he's a carefree neighbor who has stopped by to borrow some underpants. Luckily the gang member has an emergency backup labeling system applied directly to his body in the form of gang-related tattoos. If you see a tattoo of a butterfly or a rose, you're probably safe. Anything with teardrops, skulls, guns, lightning bolts, demons, or gang names—particularly if they cover the entire torso—is your signal to run.

9

Financial Weasels

Wherever there is money, there are weasels, usually in direct proportion. Someday an economist will win the Nobel Prize for discovering the exact dollar-per-weasel equation that explains our world. It will look something like this:

1 Weasel = $10

In other words, wherever there is anything of value worth $10, a weasel will appear as if by magic. Twenty dollars means two weasels, and so on. This explains why banks have so many employees (i.e., weasels) even though the entire banking system could be computerized and run by three people. Most of the banking weasels are employed solely to keep the other weasels from stealing all the money. Banks use a sophisticated system of weasel-cancellation technology, such as requiring at least two weasels to be in the vault area at all times. The assumption is that any bank employee left alone with piles of cash for more than ten seconds would start shoving handfuls into her panties.

Weasels are attracted to money like flies to unwashed monkeys. That's why the floor of the New York Stock Exchange is so crowded.* You know there's lots of money involved because the people are willing to put up with such bad conditions. Imagine showing up for that job interview.

Interviewer: "Your job is to wake up at three A.M., drive for an hour, then stand in a crowd of tense, shouting men, on a floor covered with garbage. You will be tense and shouting too, all day, every business day. No sitting down. And the bond traders have to wear clown jackets."

It's a hideous job, but still there is no shortage of weasels to fill the room to capacity every day. Weasels follow the money. If you took that same amount of money and sealed it in drums and dropped it in the ocean, 4 billion weasels would drown just trying to be near it.

The entire financial system is designed to transfer money from lesser weasels to greater weasels. Someday, if everything goes according to plan, one supreme weasel will have all of the money and everyone else will be his or her domestic servant. I hope I get the top job because I'm not good at housework.**

*In case I lost you on the analogy, I mean there are lots of people at the New York Stock Exchange because there is lots of money involved, not because they like to be around unwashed monkeys, although they do.

**When I do my laundry, I always mix the colored clothes with my white gym socks. It seems to me that if the washing machine can clean dirt from my socks, then it can also clean the colored dye off them. Now all my socks are the color of a dead tuna, but I'm optimistic that the next washing will fix that.

But judging from my history of investing, I'm not destined to be the supreme financial weasel. I've actively invested in the stock market since 1980. Since then I have amassed gains of zero. I keep telling myself that I'm investing "for the long term," which I define as several million years.

My problem is that I listen to financial experts (i.e., greater weasels), who give valuable advice for moving my money from me to them. My first clue that the experts are less than omnipotent might have been that they all recommend different and conflicting things. The one thing that all of their recommendations have in common is that if you follow their advice, they will get richer.

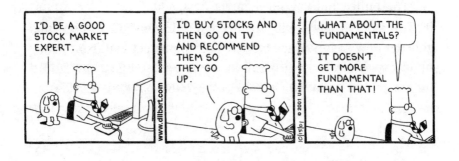

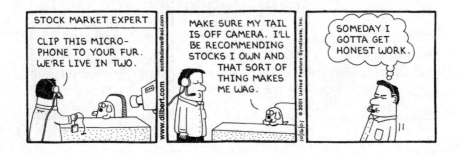

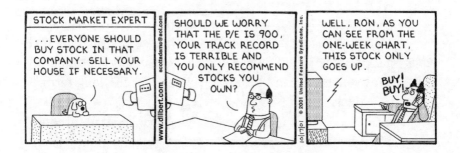

Professional stock analysts can do something that you can't do on your own, and that is to talk directly to the senior management of a company. That's how a stock analyst gets all the important inside scoop not available to the general public, including important CEO quotes like this:

"The future looks good!"

The stock analyst will sell that valuable insight to you, the ignorant and unsophisticated investor, to protect you from yourself. Most of the time the analyst will tell you to buy the stock. But if a company doesn't use the investment-banking services of the analyst's firm, then the stock is rated "underperform" and you shouldn't buy it.

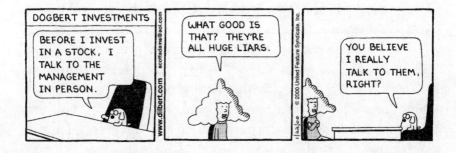

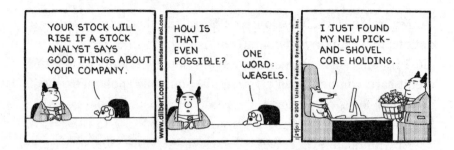

The scary thing is that although I don't know much about investing, chances are that I know more than you. So as a public service I will give you a brief tutorial of the world of financial weasels.

Credit Cards

Credit cards are the crack cocaine of the financial world. They start out as a no-fee, low-interest way to get instant gratification, but the next thing you know you're freebasing shoes at Nordstrom. Credit cards are very profitable for banks because bankers understand that people are both greedy and bad at math. This is the same knowledge used by scam artists, with the important distinction that scam artists don't charge penalties if you pay them late.

I use a credit card that earns airline miles every time I use it. At first I thought those suckers were giving me something for nothing. I enjoyed knowing that with every purchase I was ripping them off. But I noticed they kept mailing me the bill very near the due date—which caused me to pay late every month—which meant I paid late fees every month—which means it will cost me about $12,000 to get a free plane ticket to San Diego.

My credit card bills come stuffed with so many offers and options that I am mystified and confused by it all. I think that if I die in some sort of freakish travel-related accident, then the credit card company will give me discounts on appliances. Or if an airline loses my luggage, I get free long-distance phone calls, but only for incoming calls. I don't remember the details.

Any financial expert will tell you that keeping a balance on a credit card is the worst financial move you can make. The only thing worse is paying a financial planner to tell you not to keep a balance on your credit card. That's like giving yourself a wedgie and then paying someone to tell you it was a bad idea.

Financial Planners

I once tried to write a book about personal investing. It was supposed to be geared toward younger people who were investing for the first time. After extensive research on all topics related to personal investing, I realized I had a problem. I could describe everything that a young first-time investor needs to know on one page. No one wants to buy a one-page book even if that page is well written. As a consumer you'd feel you were paying mostly for the binding. If God materialized on earth and wrote the secret of the universe on one page, he wouldn't be able to get a publisher. People would look at it and say, "That's all well and good, but I'm paying mostly for the cover."

If you want to yank the chain of your financial planner, I'll give you my one-page summary of investing (for U.S. citizens), below. Make a copy and bring it with you to your next meeting. Nothing is more annoying to a highly trained professional than seeing his or her entire body of knowledge on one page. There's no joke here, except for the one that's on you if you pay for this sort of advice.

Everything You Need to Know about Personal Investing

Make a will.

Pay off your credit card balance.

Get term life insurance if you have a family to support.

Fund your company 401K to the maximum.

Fund your IRA to the maximum.

Buy a house if you want to live in a house and can afford it.

Put six months' expenses in a money market account.

Take whatever money is left over and invest 70 percent in a stock index fund and 30 percent in a bond fund through any discount brokerage company and never touch it until retirement.

If any of this confuses you, or you have something special going on (retirement, college planning, tax issue), hire a fee-based financial planner, not one who charges a percentage of your portfolio.

Everything else you might want to do with your money is a bad idea compared to what's on my one-page summary. You want an annuity? It's worse. You want a whole life insurance policy? It's worse. You want to invest in individual stocks? It's worse. You want a managed mutual fund instead of an index fund? It's worse. I could go on, but you get the point.

Here's a fun conversation to have with your financial planner at your next meeting.

> *You:* Stock index funds have done well in the past. Shouldn't I put most of my money there and not pay you anything for managing my money?
>
> *Financial Planner:* No. Past performance is not a good predictor of the future.
>
> *You:* Aren't all of your recommendations based on past performance?
>
> *Financial Planner:* Yes, but that's different because . . . interest rates . . . um . . . tax issues . . . um . . . hey, do you think it's going to rain? It looks cloudy.
>
> *You:* So if I shouldn't use past performance as my guide, I might as well pick a strategy that has never worked, right?
>
> *Financial Planner:* Shut up.

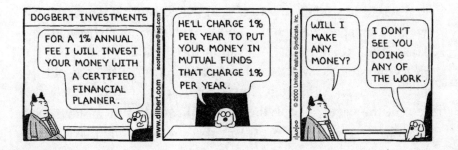

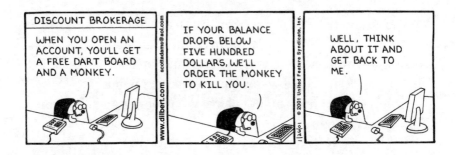

Talking-Head Weasels

I enjoy watching TV shows that feature weasels predicting the future of the economy. Most of the talking-head weasels predict that the economy will improve in "six to twelve months." That's a safe prediction because no one will remember what you said, it might actually turn out to be right, and it makes you sound like an upbeat optimist who should be invited back to the show. The producers of financial TV shows prefer optimistic guests because it makes the viewers feel good. If too many pessimists get on TV, then the viewers will get depressed and start watching *Oprah*.

This is another case where weasels make the world a better place for all of us. The last thing you'd want is honesty when it comes to predicting the economy. If all the experts came on TV and said, "The economy is going to hell. You'll be living in a cardboard box in six months," that would cause a panic, people would stop spending money, and the whole economy would collapse. With the current TV ratio of three optimistic weasels for every pessimistic weasel, all viewpoints are considered but no one gets hurt. Essentially, four producers at CNBC control the fate of the earth. I hope they don't all wake up in a bad mood one day.

10

Airline Weasels

I think you'll agree that no book is complete without a mongoose analogy. (If you disagree, I'd hate to see the garbage *you've* been reading.)

Mongoose analogy: A mongoose is to a snake what a paranoid is to a weasel.

In other words, the paranoid is the natural enemy of the human weasel.* The weasel depends on his victims to be gullible. Most people let down their guard sooner or later. But paranoid people have total protection around the clock. They see your conspiracies before you even plan them.

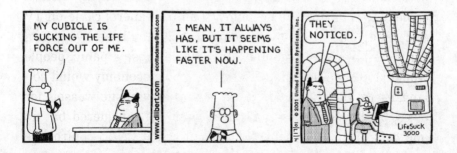

*The sign of a good analogy is that you have to explain it.

I'm paranoid and proud of it. I have lots of conspiracy theories that I call *facts* because *hallucinations* has a bad connotation.

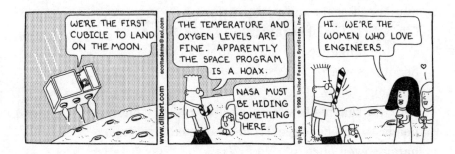

One of my theories is that a single holding company owns every airline in the world. Granted, all of the "competing" airline companies have different uniforms and logos. (How hard would it be to fake that?) But they all fly the same kind of planes and they all use the same airports. That's a little *too* coincidental. And if that's not enough to convince you, look at the first letter in each of these airline names:

Southwest

United

Canada Air

KLA

Eastern

Russian Airlines

That's right—it spells SUCKER.

Would a "real" competitive industry hire ex-convicts to handle your luggage, make you wait two hours for your flight, give you a seat that's designed for a hobbit, sell more tickets than the number of seats and pay the extra people to get off the plane? C'mon! That's not even trying!

And don't get me started about the seat belts. If my plane is heading toward the side of a mountain, I'm not going to be thinking, "Phew! I'm glad I'm securely fastened!" They try to tell you the seat belts are to prevent people from bonking their heads on the ceiling in case of turbulence. I've never seen that happen even once, but I'd like to.

Hey, if it's wrong to fantasize about people bonking their heads on the ceiling, then I don't want to be right. In my defense, I only wish for the bonking to happen to people who annoy me. My growing list includes these offenders:

1. The baby that's currently kicking the back of my seat all the way from San Francisco to New York City.

2. And its mother.

3. The guy who didn't bring a book and figures he'll talk to me every few minutes for the next six hours. I hope he's not reading the screen on my laptop right now.

4. The guy who boarded the plane last, opened the overhead bin where my carry-on luggage was cowering in fear, then crushed it with his bulging, testosterone-laced bag of anvils.

If you've ever flung pencils into ceiling tiles, that's the vision I have. I imagine each of these offenders being launched by turbulence into the bulkhead, sticking by their pointy heads, and kicking their legs in a way that seems at first shocking but eventually causes everyone to laugh and order more beverages.

Speaking of beverages, why do the airlines always fill you with drinks and then turn on the seat belt sign? Those beverages have to go someplace, and when your pores are as clogged as mine, that doesn't leave many options. Sometimes the airline just teases you. You sit there all bloated on diet Coke, staring at the seat belt sign like a dog with a biscuit on his nose, waiting for the "no seat belt" beep. Two things you don't want to hear on a long flight are "Here's your third diet Coke, Mr. Adams," and "It looks like we'll have turbulence. Keep the seat belt snug across your bladder for the next five hours."

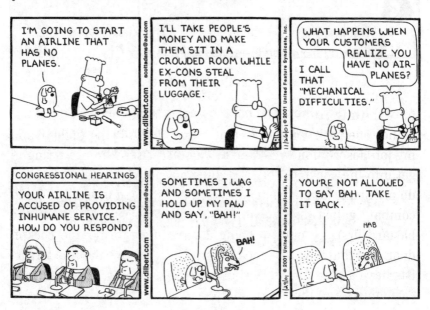

Airlines have the best weasel excuses of any business. If they forget to schedule a flight crew for your flight, that's "mechanical difficulties." No one is going to argue about mechanical difficulties because winning that argument would look like this:

Airline Employee: Okay, sir. Have it your way. We'll put that plane in the air right away. But if the wing falls off in flight, we expect you to punch a hole in the window, stick out your arm, and start flapping.

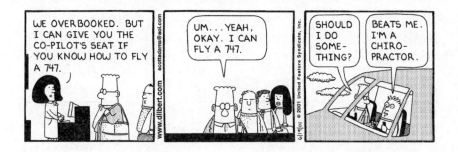

Now I'm preparing for another cross-country flight and I have the misfortune of being assigned a seat near the front of the plane. The cashews up there are terrific, but being male, it's in my job description to leap onto any terrorists who are trying to get into the cockpit. This is a dilemma because while I want to do my manly and patriotic duty, I'm not so good in hand-to-hand combat against highly trained suicide terrorists. If I get to the bastard first, I'll end up being a battering ram for the cockpit door, and that won't be good for anyone. I'm sure that the terrorists have a plan for every contingency—including attack by frail cartoonists—and have special maneuvers to deal with it.

So I've been practicing my own move that I call the "pulled hamstring." That's the one where I yell, "Stand back, citizens! I'll get him!" Then I take one step and fall to the floor clutching my hamstring. As the other passengers surge forward to join the battle, I fold into a ball and roll under a seat. I plan to wear a shirt that has a luggage handle on the back so I look exactly like a carry-on bag. I hope no one puts a bag of anvils on me.

11

Marketing Weasels

Marketing is a dark science devoted to making people want things they don't need. It's second on the list of Top Ten All-Time Evils.

Top Ten All-Time Evils

1. Leadership
2. **Marketing**
3. Satan
4. Human Resources
5. Cannibalism
6. Decaffeinated coffee
7. Death squads
8. Three-hour meetings
9. Cats
10. Hitler

Research

Step one in marketing is to do research to learn what customers want. Step two is to ignore what people want and try to package whatever it is that your company knows how to make. That's called product development.

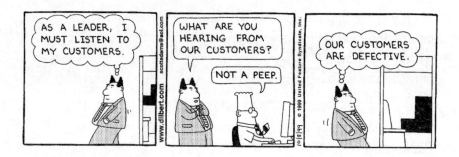

In some rare cases a company is capable of making a product that customers want. The business term for that is "I'll be damned, they actually buy this crap." Alternatively, if you are the marketing manager in charge of product development, you might call it "an accomplishment." Whatever you call it, it's rare. The normal situation is that a company squints and strains and grunts out whatever its disinterested employees are capable of producing. Then the marketing people put a bow on it and tell the unsuspecting public that it's exactly what they want.

You aren't born knowing what you want. It's marketing's job to tell you. Most of what you are told bounces right off, but sometimes a bit of it sticks and collectively forms what is known as your "personality." But that's a whole other book.

Channel Strategy

Channel is a fancy word for "where you sell your product." Your company will hire a channel manager who will hold many meetings to brainstorm channel strategy. He will collect all the valuable input and then recommend the same channel strategy he used in his last job because that's all he knows how to do.

If you are in a large company, some sucker on your payroll will get the job of selling your company's products to other employees within the company. If, by some gigantic stroke of luck, your company makes the best products of their kind, then this is an easy job. In every other case it's a form of employee abuse.

Packaging

Few things are more important to the success of a product than packaging. I'm not too proud to admit that I'll buy anything that comes in a nice package, as long as it's also overpriced. I figure if a company can make a good package, it probably does other things well too. The package and the price are usually all I know about a product before I buy it. That system has worked pretty well for me so far. Sure, everything I own is defective, but so is everything you own, and I don't spend as much time shopping.

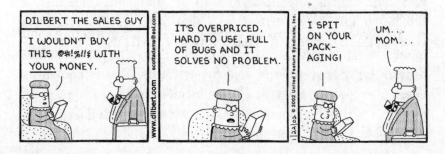

Pricing

At some point in product development, the marketing professional needs to set a price. The price should be high enough to make a profit and low enough that your lazy and timid customers won't bother to demand a refund.

Most companies have a profit margin that is nearly the same as the percentage of unhappy customers who didn't bother to complain. Let's say, for example, you sell shirts and you earn about 20 percent after expenses. According to my theory, that means about 20 percent of your customers take your shirts home and find out that all the buttons fall off in the laundry. If all unhappy consumers demanded refunds, the entire system of capitalism would collapse.* Fortunately most people are timid and lazy. So the next time you see a timid and lazy person, walk right up and thank him for doing nothing and saving the economy. He'll beam with pride and then hide behind something until you go away.

Advertising

The Greek philosophers believed the universe was composed of just three basic elements: weasels, crap, and dirt. If I may borrow their colorful lingo, allow me to say that sometimes there's too much dirt between the crap that you're selling and the weasels that might buy it. That's why you need advertising.

---

*Yes, I know the math doesn't work. But sometimes truth must be sacrificed to make excellent points.

There are three kinds of products vis-à-vis* your competition:

1. Better crap

2. Exactly the same crap

3. Crappier crap

If your product is better than your competitor's, charge a higher price and act arrogant. Sometimes, just for fun, announce a new version of your product, take advance orders, and don't produce anything. Or do what trendy dance clubs do and only sell your product to people who are attractive and fashionable. That will create an artificial demand. Artificial demand is what makes diamonds so valuable. To put this in perspective, if there were only one rabbit left in the whole world, rabbit crap would be worth more than diamonds. That's just something to think about the next time you get engaged.

BMW once suggested in their ads that their cars have a soul. Personally, I hope they don't. I'd be so mad if I got to heaven** and Saint Peter told me heaven was full because they started taking BMWs.

> ***Saint Peter:*** Sorry, man. We gave our last cloud to a 325is.
> ***Me:*** I don't need a cloud. I can sit anywhere. Really.

---

*Hey, I used *vis-à-vis* in a sentence and I'm not even French!

**This example dialogue that features me getting to heaven assumes that God is omnipotent in every way except for knowing what I write in my books.

> ***Saint Peter:***   All we have left is some cigar smoke and a fart
> that won't go away.
> ***Me:***   What kind of fart?

Being overpriced won't hurt sales because some people are genetically incapable of buying anything but the most expensive products. I'm one of those people. In my case it's not snobbery so much as laziness and a bone-deep hatred of shopping. If I'm looking at two items and one costs more, I assume the expensive one does the most or lasts the longest, especially if the package is nicely done. I know that if I buy the cheap one, and I find out later it doesn't have the features I need, then I'll have to return it and buy the good one. *That's twice as much shopping!* I consider the extra amount that I pay for "the good one" a sort of anti-shopping insurance. Some might call it a tax on idiots. Same thing.

If your product is exactly the same as your competitor's product, then you need to mislead without lying, i.e., weasel-words.

For example: "No product has been proven more effective." That's a clever way of saying "These products are identical" or possibly "This product has never been compared to anything in a controlled study." You can use that same technique in your professional life because chances are that you've never been compared to competent employees in any sort of controlled experiment. Your résumé could say, "No employee has ever been proven to be smarter or more attractive" or "No one has been proven to embezzle less!"

Brochure

If you want a customer to buy a *little bit* of whatever you're selling, you need to communicate the merits of your product in a clear and simple way. But if you want customers to buy *vast quantities* of your product, then it's a good idea to thoroughly mislead them. To do that you'll need a brochure.

Brochure: Proof that cameras lie.

I am convinced that a skilled photographer could stick a camera up a mosquito's butt, snap a few rolls, and use Photoshop to make it look like the Grand Ballroom at Windsor Palace.

The Old Fakeroo

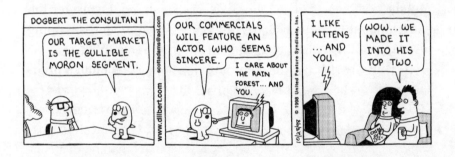

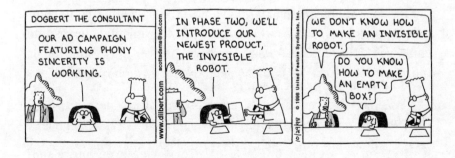

I just saw an advertisement for a bank that says it cares about customers as *people,* not numbers. Apparently that bank does a better job screening prospective employees than those banks that offered me jobs. When I worked at a bank, the only time I ever cared about a customer was when he was complaining to my supervisor about me. And then I wanted him dead, so I'm not sure that counts as "caring" in the TV commercial way.

Advertising is different from lying because no one is expected to believe advertisements, except for extremely gullible people. And it's generally agreed that the "gullible people" market segment has no hope of holding on to its money anyway. So it's pretty much first come, first served as far as robbing the gullible.

People are getting better at ignoring advertisements. So advertisers are working harder at ambushing us. My favorite advertising tricks are the Web ads that dupe you into thinking you need to click on a button in order to:

- Speed up your computer

- Claim your prize

- Destroy a computer virus

- Check a message

And then, surprise! It's only an advertisement.

You have to wonder what advertisers will try next. I predict that someday a baby will latch onto its mother's breast, expecting to get some delicious lunch, only to discover that he's wrestling with a fake breast that activates an advertisement for Pampers.

This lunch is brought to you by Pampers. Push the round button for more information.

Using a fake breast to advertise to babies will seem "over the line" for about a month and then we'll all get used to it.

Revenge

Nothing motivates a consumer more than an opportunity to give the shaft to a retailer or vendor. Consumers are so used to being on the receiving end of the screwing that they are blinded by any chance for revenge. A clever advertiser can take advantage of that impulse this way.

From the mailbag:

Dear Mr. Adams,

I have a friend who owns a music store. He had several copies of an album that wasn't selling well. So he put all of the copies next to each other on the shelf and labeled them all $16.99 except one, which he labeled $15.99. $15.99 was the actual price he wanted for the album, but on the shelf it looked like a mistake. After a sale, he would quietly replace one of the $16.99 tags with a $15.99 tag. Sales of the album increased. People were buying the thing simply because they thought they were screwing him.

What impresses me is not so much the shrewdness of this scheme, but my friend's acceptance of the fact that people go out of their way to screw him.

Testimonials

I was shocked—simply shocked!—when I heard that a major movie studio had been making up fake quotes to advertise its bad movies. Since then the studios have cleaned up their act and only use "real" quotes. Just last night I saw a TV ad for an upcoming movie. The bold quote on the bottom of the screen was something like "most exciting movie of the year!" Below the quote was a tiny white smudge that I believe was the name of whoever said it. I looked closely to see if the smudge was some sort of word or letters, and I'm pretty sure it's just a smudge. That's all I needed to know. If a tiny white smudge liked the movie, it must be a winner!

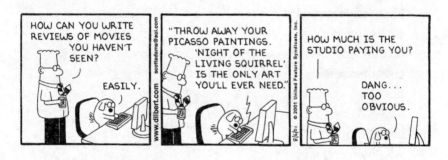

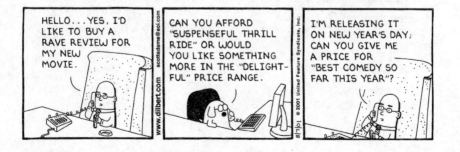

Customer Retention

The best customers are the ones who can't figure out how to stop sending you money. If you want to attract that kind of customer, you need to offer a service that can't be seen or touched, like insurance or Internet connectivity. That way, you and your employees can dissolve into the background never to be seen or contacted again. The only evidence of your existence is the continuous billing or—better yet—automatic deduction from the customer's checking account.

Dear Mr. Adams,

I needed to cancel my Internet service. The company doesn't allow you to do it by e-mail or Web although you can sign up that way. You need a certified letter or you need to call customer service. I tried calling them fifteen times over the past four weeks but couldn't handle the thirty-minute wait times. Twice their system disconnected me after waiting fifteen minutes. They have a meter on their Web site telling you their wait times—which they recently disabled. This morning I got through after forty minutes of waiting. Their message announced that today the wait times were "over ten minutes."

12

Sales Weasels

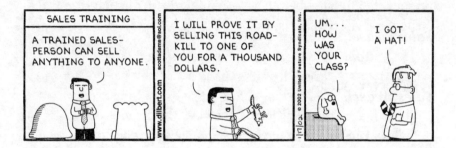

Marketing would be nothing without their winged monkeys, the salespeople. Salespeople know that the human brain has several parts. One part of your brain—the rational part—thinks, "All I need is some food and shelter, maybe some sex, and I'm good to go. That's all I need." That part of the brain doesn't want to buy rubber hamsters that sing when you clap. The job of the salesperson is to deactivate that happy part of the brain and get to the part that thinks, "Unless I buy an unending stream of unnecessary merchandise, I will die."

The first task of a salesman is to make you miserable, because happy people don't need anything. If there's nothing wrong with you, the salesperson will provide you with a problem. Salespeople want you to think about how desperately inadequate your life is now and how wonderful life will be in the future, assuming you buy some unnecessary products.

Technique is everything. A smart salesperson never uses the word *no* because it might get you thinking it's okay to use that word yourself. Instead, the sales weasel will reword your question to something that can be answered with a yes.

Example:

You:	Do you have one of these items in stock?
Sales Weasel:	Yes, we usually do.
You:	I didn't ask your *probability* of having it. I asked if you *do* have it.
Sales Weasel:	Yes, I can check as soon as your credit card clears.
You:	You keep slightly changing my question so you can answer yes!
Sales Weasel:	Yes, I am. You're welcome.

At some point in the sales process the sales weasel must give you information about the product, including its price. The sales weasel prefers to give you information about the product after the sale, when it can do the least harm. The undisputed experts at this method are insurance salespeople. They have the advantage of using fear to make you act irrationally.

You:	May I see a copy of the insurance policy before deciding whether to buy it?
Insurance Salesman:	We send you the details of what you purchased ninety days after you sign up.
You:	Um . . . but how do I know what I'm buying?

Insurance	I told you: it's coverage for this and that and
Salesman:	so forth and so on, et cetera. I don't see how I
	can be more specific.
You:	Still, I'd like to see a policy first.
Insurance	*You're gonna die! Your house will burn down!*
Salesman:	*Robbers are circling your block! Sign it! Sign*
	it! Sign it, you fool!

Every sales weasel will tell you his product is less expensive than the alternative. The sales weasel's secret weapon is to carefully choose the comparison. For example, a Mercedes-Benz is less expensive than a Volkswagen Beetle if you compare the entire cost of the Beetle to the floor mats of the Mercedes. While this sounds like outright lying, it's still within the allowable zone if, when challenged, the salesperson can say it with a straight face and a wide-eyed dopey look that says, "Yes, I suppose you might look at it another way. It's exactly that sort of diversity of opinion that makes life so wonderful."

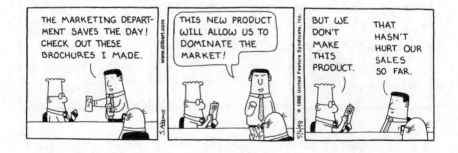

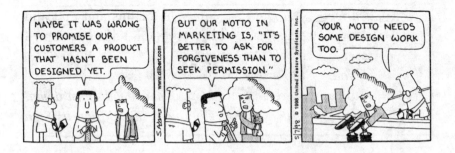

In many ways the easiest product to sell is one that doesn't exist. Things that don't exist are not defective nor can they have bad word of mouth. In fact, nonexistent things are nearly always perfect. Sometimes you have to average out the defectiveness of your current version of your product by promising that the next upgrade—the one that doesn't exist—is perfect. When you combine defective and perfect, you get "pretty good," and that's way better than what most of us are used to.

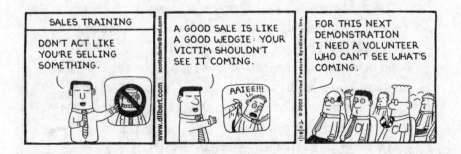

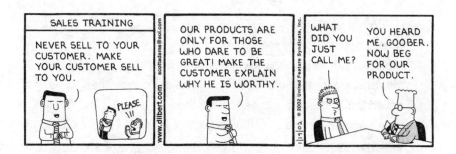

There's a fine line between ordinary selling and outright scamming. The people who ignore that line are sometimes referred to as "successful" and can be found anywhere, including in front of your building, as in this example.

Dear Mr. Adams,

One persistent "weasel scam" I've seen (and my wife was taken in by) is the "broken freezer unit, thawing meat" routine.

A pickup truck with a freezer unit in the bed shows up outside your business or residence. The driver explains that the freezer unit has just gone dead, and he's got a whole load of meat in there that's going to spoil if he can't find somebody to take it. He offers you an "at cost" deal on a box or two of prime steaks, if you've got space in your freezer or can get them home in time. Of course, HE can't get back to his own office in time to save them.

It's surprising how well this works; he's very slick, and he plays on the natural desire to get a good deal while also helping the guy out and avoiding a waste of good food.

What you get for your money is a batch of overpriced hamburger. My wife was taken in by this, but quickly realized that there were some holes in the story. She called me, and we immediately put a stop on the check, then called their "office" and explained that we decided we didn't need their meat. But as a courtesy we'd keep it frozen and they could either pick it up at their leisure, or we'd deliver it to their office.

They've been running the same scam in town for at least eight to ten years, spreading it around so they don't show up any one place too often.

Have you ever seen a cow surrounded by flies? It uses its tail all day long to ward them off. That's how you feel if your job involves making any sort of purchases for the company. Salespeople will be swarming over you. If you're lucky enough to have a secretary, then you can delegate the swatting. Or if the secretary is a weasel, it looks more like this:

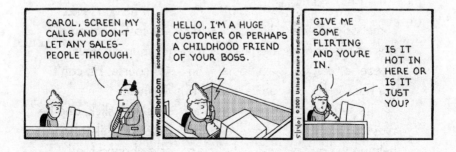

Retail Sales Weasels

It's not easy working in the retail sales profession, but there is one huge weasel advantage worth noting: there's no fear of losing your job. You can always get another unpleasant retail job across the street. That's a huge psychological advantage, weasel-wise. It's like having a superpower.

There are two types of retail weasels:

Unscrupulous (i.e., paid on commission)

Lazy (i.e., paid by the hour)

Unscrupulous employees, who are paid on commission, have to screw their customers and coworkers to make money. The lazy ones only screw their employer. If you have a choice, try to get a job as a lazy employee because, as the name implies, it's easier.

The most important skill for the retail weasel is telling the difference between a serious buyer and a looky-loo. If you're working on commission, you want to pounce on any serious buyers like a dog on an ass-flavored biscuit. But if you're working for a plain old salary, you want to avoid the serious shoppers—the ones who create extra work—and focus on the looky-loos. Smile at them and offer your service, your knowledge, your undying energy, and your sacred honor to help them find the right product. When the looky-loo says, "No thanks. I'm just looking," it's okay for you to think, "Whew," but you should say something like "If you need anything at all, just ask."

One foolproof way to lower your workload is to avoid stocking popular items. I know that sounds more like a comic than real life, but it's been my experience that salaried employees of retail stores go out of their way to avoid carrying popular items. For example, my local sneaker store never has my size (the most common men's size) in good sneakers because, as a salaried employee explained to me, "People keep buying them." The employees seem entirely content in not carrying desirable products because in their case it means touching fewer feet.

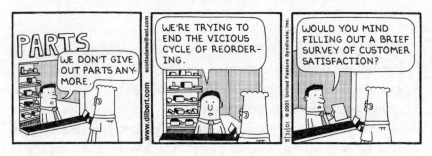

13

CEO Weasels

When you have mastered the weasel techniques in this book, you will probably be asked to run a major corporation. That's when you need a whole new set of weasel tools that are specific to the CEO job. In this chapter I will give you a brief tutorial for handling your new CEO assignment.

On your first day of work as a CEO make sure you clamp down on any announcements of good news that might be in the pipeline. You want to save good news for later, when you can take credit. The first year of your reign should be nonstop bad news. Take massive write-offs as soon as possible. It will look as if you're "sweeping out the barn" and making strategic changes. But more importantly it lowers your profits so that after you "correct all the mistakes of the last CEO," the first full year under your leadership will show a huge increase in profit, even if nothing actually improved. As a secondary benefit, it makes the prior CEO look like a chimp.

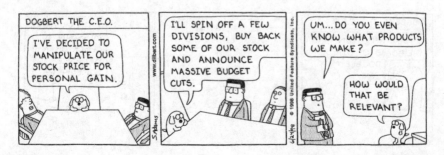

You might also need to jigger the books to make it appear that sales for your most important products are improving during your watch. Here's one way to do it:

> Dear Mr. Adams,
>
> Our management had a brain wave recently. They needed to increase the sales of one of our leading products. They succeeded. How you ask? Easy, they just slapped the product name on all our other products. It's devilish with a dash of manic genius.

As CEO, be sure to take control of the board of directors. Maneuver your buddies into any openings and conspire to kick off anyone who might be a threat to your compensation. Recommend a big increase in pay for directors. They'll return the favor later by voting for a huge compensation package for you. As a general rule, it's good to have the sort of job where you can recommend pay increases for the people who recommend pay increases for you.

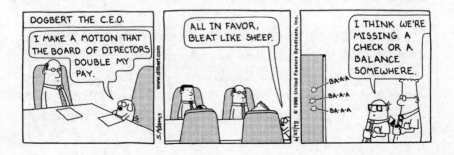

You'll need some sort of cover story for why you should get paid ten thousand times more than the average worker in your company. The best excuse is that much of your pay is "at risk" in the form of stock options, whereas the minimum-wage employee is pretty much guaranteed his poverty-level paycheck, at least until you downsize him to increase the value of your stock options. But you don't need to mention that last part.

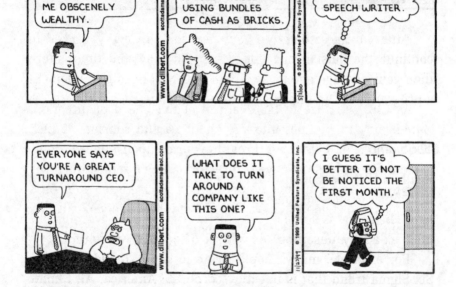

The great thing about stock options is that they don't need to be valuable forever—just long enough for you to cash them out. So as CEO you only need the stock to appreciate once during your reign and you'll be rich for life. You can make that happen by firing a bunch of people after your options vest. Wall Street

loves cost cutting. If that doesn't work, try merging with someone. If that doesn't work, just lie about your company's future.
There's no law against optimism.

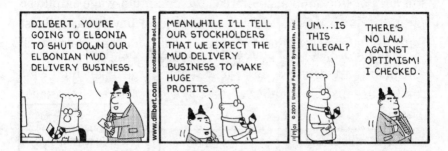

After you've settled into your new job as CEO, you need to
continue the illusion of being worth ten thousand times more
than your average employee. To do that, you need to implement
a program with an impressive-sounding name such as . . .

Six Sigma

Readers of Dilbert often wonder how I can be so insightful about
new office trends despite having left cubicle life several years
ago. The secret is simple: I assume everyone in the world is like
me, i.e., a lazy, unscrupulous weasel. The rest flows naturally.

For example, many people wrote to say I should mock the
Six Sigma trend that is infecting corporate America. All I knew
about Six Sigma was this:

- Consultants were involved.

- The employees who are trained in the process are awarded
  karate-like titles such as green belt, brown belt, black belt.

- GE and Motorola were two companies that used Six Sigma.

- It's a process for identifying and eliminating errors or defects or bad things in general.

From those clues I could deduce a great deal. First, because consultants are involved, and consultants charge by the hour, you can be sure that the number of meetings increases exponentially.

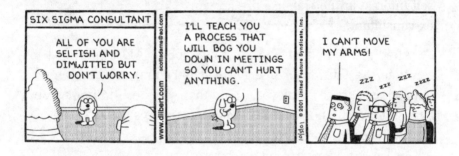

Consultants have to sell their services to get in the door. That means they must convince senior management that Six Sigma is "new" and that companies that use it do better than those that don't. That argument always goes something like this:

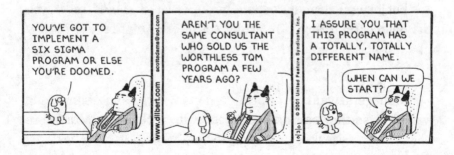

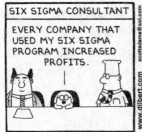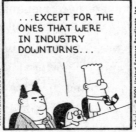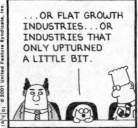

Maybe you don't think consultants would act in their own self-interest at the expense of the client. Here's a story from one ex-consultant.

Dear Mr. Adams,

I worked at a consulting company. We were measured on "utilization," which is the percentage of your time billed out to customers. I had a project that I completed in half the estimated time. My reward? My management was mad at me because I didn't bill as many hours as I could have, and that hurt my utilization numbers. So I asked them, "You mean by doing a good job, I'm going to get a bad rating, but if I were slow, stupid, and took four times as long, I'd get a good rating?" They said, "Essentially, yes."

Managers want to appear as if they are doing something valuable, so they can be promoted to higher-paying jobs where they can pretend to do even more valuable things. As an executive weasel it's always a good idea to "roll out a program" with a cool name and hope something lucky happens in the industry so you can take credit. Business reporters love writing stories about programs that seem to improve profits—because other weasel managers will want to read those stories and copy the weasel techniques and get in magazines themselves. Capitalism depends heavily on magazines.

If you're a weasel manager, you hope your company doesn't improve on your first day of work when all you've done so far is eat a doughnut and take a spectacular three-minute wizz in the executive washroom to mark your territory. You'll have to claim that whatever you did on the first day caused the spike in sales. If you find yourself in this situation, I recommend that you give credit to the doughnut and not the other thing.

After you take credit for implementing a spiffy new program that appears to have increased profits, you will be rewarded with raises and bonuses and media accolades. At that point you're pretty much screwed unless you continue doing whatever program you credited for "turning around the company."

When I heard that GE and Motorola were using Six Sigma, I knew it must be the sort of virus that prefers a large bureaucratic host—the kind of place where it's unwise to be the one to identify a "problem" with the current way of doing things. And when I heard about the funny language (people earn black belts), I knew that the employees would have the attitude expressed by Alice in this comic:

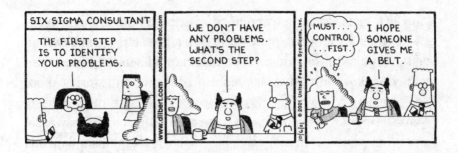

Once you have your Six Sigma program in place, you can take credit for any lucky thing that happens in the industry while blaming the industry itself for any unlucky things.

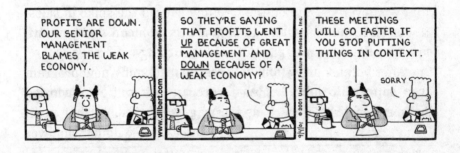

CEO Exit Strategy

If, despite all your random reorganizations and selfish actions, the company continues to do poorly, and you've already cashed out a lot of your stock options during one of the up years, you might have some pressure on you from stockholders. They will be clambering for a new CEO who can write off your mistakes and do some mergers to get the stock price up again. Since you know that the stock will probably go up again no matter who is the CEO, you want to postpone your demise long enough to be there when it happens and get another unearned truckload of cash. If you're in the midst of downsizing and salary freezes, volunteer to share the pain, like this:

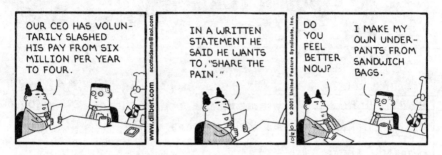

As CEO you're usually among the first to know when your company's in a death spiral. If you're smart, you'll leave before the news breaks, using your "successful track record" to land an even better CEO job at another company where your buddies, the board of directors, are also serving as board members.

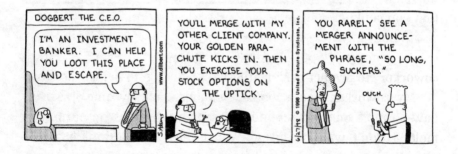

14

Social Weaseling

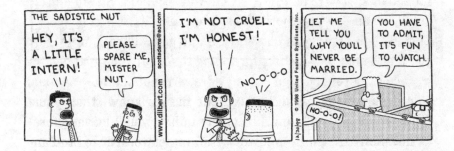

In my entire life I have only met one person who could "handle the truth" as Jack Nicholson once said in a movie. By that I mean that you could give this one unique person a brutally frank criticism about anything from her looks to her personality and she would sincerely appreciate it. I will refer to her as "my coworker" to protect her identity.

My coworker was a woman who had exactly one physical flaw—a mole on the back of her neck. But this was no ordinary mole. I don't want to exaggerate its size, but I think it was attending trade school at night.

Anyway, my coworker often stated that she wanted honesty at all times, no matter the cost. Most people say they want the truth, but they don't really. I thought my coworker was full of it too. But over time, and after seeing some examples where it seemed to be true, I started to think she might actually prefer hearing the truth.

That's when I mentioned the mole. I told her I couldn't understand why an attractive woman would want a full-scale replica of Saddam Hussein on her neck. Then I rolled into a defensive ball and waited to be pummeled.

But the beating didn't come. She casually explained that the mole had always been there, so she was used to it. It had started small, when she was born, then had used "weasel creep"—see page 53—to grow to its current size and geopolitical power.

True to her word, she appreciated the truth and arranged for a doctor to remove the mole. As a precaution, the National Guard surrounded the hospital, but the mole didn't put up a fight. A flatbed truck hauled it away to become a tourist attraction somewhere in the Midwest. And my coworker thanked me for being the first person in her entire life to mention the mole.

Obviously my coworker is a wonderful oddity. For the other six billion people on earth it is better to avoid the truth—or at least weasel it—whenever possible, or else you get this situation:

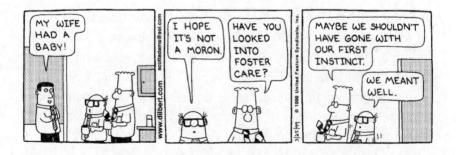

Avoiding People over Forty

Never ask anyone over the age of forty "How are you?" or "What's new?" or anything of that nature. In fact, you should avoid any sort of conversation with that segment of the population, including me. What you'll get is an unending description of medical crises, mental fluctuations, and bodily secretions that would make a taxidermist squirm. When the forty-plus person is done talking about his own health problems, he'll move on to those of his parents, spouse, coworkers, and pets. When you're over forty, even your dog needs a new hip.

Asking about Work

The worst thing to ask at a party is "How's the job?" That's an invitation to boredom so severe that your brain will crawl down the inside of your spine and try to escape out of your colon. If you feel the need to ask someone about his job, make sure he's over forty. That way there's a good chance the story will get cut short by some sort of convulsions.

Hair Compliments

No one will ever tell you that your haircut looks like the product of an ill-advised love affair between Don King and a moldy cantaloupe. All you hear about your own hair are weasel compliments. In your heart you know it can't be true that *every time* you change your hairstyle it looks *better.* If that were true, you'd change your hair every day. It would look better and better until eventually you could blind people with your beauty.

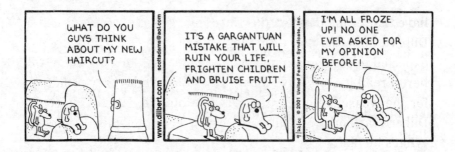

To me, women's haircuts always look bad when they're new. That's doubly true if the woman has recently married and is making the plunge to "married hair." Within six months after marriage most women opt for hairstyles that are "more convenient." The word *convenient* comes from an Elbonian word that means "looks exactly like a man, but inexplicably has breasts."

If you take any mammal and make it more "convenient," it will start to resemble an adult human male. Men are models of convenience: no makeup, no heels, no panty hose, willing to use any upholstered surface as a napkin.

When a woman with newly coiffed married-hair corners me, and I have to comment on the new look, I usually make loud comments about efficiency, like "That looks like quite a time-saver!" or "Wow, that must take two seconds to blow-dry!" That buys me time until nearby women can hear the conversation and jump into it with a barrage of insincere compliments. Then I melt into the background.

Avoiding Compliments

Sometimes you find yourself in a situation where a compliment seems to be called for but you can't bring yourself to lie. People have that problem when they meet me. Usually they've heard of Dilbert, but often they aren't fans of the strip. They think they're expected to say something along the lines of "I'm a big fan of Dilbert. I read it every day!" But if they hate Dilbert, they usually go for the weasel detour that goes something like this: "You're the Dilbert cartoonist? Really? Have you ever met Bill Watterson? What's he like?"

Weasel Favors

If someone asks you for a favor, and it's a big imposition, don't use math to explain why you shouldn't do the favor. People don't like math with refusals.

For example, as a cartoonist I get a great deal of mail from people who request signed photos, sketches, and autographs "for their collections." The reason I can't accommodate them involves math. Autograph collectors are organized and have lists of who signs autographs by mail. One hundred and fifty million people read *Dilbert,* and if it becomes known that I sign things by mail, I would soon be spending 100 percent of my time signing things.

If I tell the truth and explain the math of the situation, I will be thought a lazy bastard who does not "appreciate his fans." If I do what famous movie stars do and hire people to answer my mail and sign my name, I'll be perpetrating a fraud. I can't win.

That's why I use the weasel method. I throw away the mail and let the sender think that maybe my publisher never forwarded it. That introduces some doubt as to whether I'm a lazy bastard or my publisher is a company full of lazy bastards. Weasonable doubt is the best I can hope for.

Weasel Advice

Weasels are always eager to give unsolicited advice on topics as diverse as romance, work, and advanced satellite telemetry. But it's not because weasels like to help. It's because when you give advice, it makes you feel wise even if you have no idea what you're talking about. You can try this experiment for yourself. The next time you're in a conversation, start spouting sagelike advice as if the other person just got out of a coma and has no memory of anything except basic language skills. You'll feel like the love child of Dear Abby and Albert Einstein, which is a great feeling until you realize what your hair must look like.

It doesn't matter if your advice is bad or even dangerous. People rarely take *good* advice, much less weasel advice. So feel free to offer your wisdom on legal, medical, and scientific issues. Most people will nod and smile politely. You'll never know how much they wish the noise coming from your mouth would stop.

Example:

Normal Person: I got a speeding ticket today.

Weasel: I recommend pleading guilty to manslaughter.

Normal Person: (smiling and nodding politely) Um, okay.

Weasel: With any luck you'll go to jail, and that's good because prisoners are always on the top of the list to receive organ transplants.

Normal Person: Um . . .

Weasel: And did you know you can use toothpaste instead of cream in your coffee and you won't have to brush after meals?

Your "Office"

If you work in a cubicle, you might occasionally find yourself exaggerating its grandeur to people who you hope will never see it. You might even refer to your cubicle as an "office." If you get caught exaggerating about your "office," you can always say it was just a choice of words and then laugh and change the subject.

If you are a normal weasel, then you probably want to give people the impression that you are a power broker and a mover and shaker who is worthy of a door. And of course you want to avoid the stigma of being a cubicle person. Why? Here are some sentences you will rarely hear:

"I want to marry him. He works in an actual cubicle!"

"I knew she was destined for greatness because she was only fifty years old and already she had her own cubicle."

"You have a cubicle? You must be some sort of genius or something!"

For maximum ambiguity, when speaking of work, use the phrase "I was at the office." That leaves some question about whether you *have* an office or you were simply *in* some sort of officelike area. Equally good are "I was working at my desk" and "I swear to God I am not as big a loser as these ill-fitting pants would suggest."

What Do You Do for a Living?

If you're a doctor or a cop, you probably enjoy it when people ask you what you do for a living. You can explain your job in one word and people respect you for it. You could be the worst doctor in the world—say a surgeon who accidentally turns people into Siamese twins about twice a week—and you would still be respected. Or you could be a cop who shoots eyewitnesses to save on paperwork. It wouldn't matter. You have a one-word job description and people will love you for it.

But if you work for a corporation, you might have to weasel-word the description of your job by referring to the company you work for instead of the job itself.

Good answer: I work for Oracle.

Bad answer: I'm an Assistant Quality Administrator for the Excellence Project.

Here's an even worse answer.

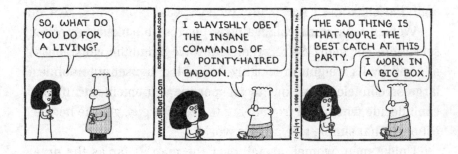

Weasel Gifts

If, despite your personality, you get invited to a party, you might be expected to bring a hostess gift. If you're a guy, you can get away with bringing something easy like some sort of mysterious liquor or dying flowers. If you want to get fancy, the general rule is that anything that has enough mass to displace water is a "gift."

If you don't want to be invited back, bring a gift that is too expensive-looking to throw away but too ugly to display. It could be some sort of candle-holding-picture-frame-vase-clock with a bag of chocolate. In all likelihood the recipient will "regift" your gift anyway. The idea with regifting is that you have a closet full of the worthless gifts that people gave to you, so when you need a gift for someone else, you just go to the closet and slap a bow on something you already have. It's like having a gift store in your house, except the store only sells gifts that no one wants.

Women have an advantage in the gift-giving area, enjoying both shopping for gifts and receiving them. The average man would rather be whacked with a ball peen hammer—on a body part that reminds him of the hammer—than shop for items to fill a gift basket.

Women have another advantage because it's much easier to select gifts for men. We're predictable. We judge the worthiness of a gift by its weight, in roughly this order: house, automobile, large-screen television, keg, tools, sporting equipment, etc. If you can't decide which tool from Sears to get for a guy, get the heaviest one. That simple rule always works.

Unlike men, women are all over the map as far as the preferred weight of their gifts. Women would rather have—against all reason—a light piece of jewelry as opposed to something substantial like a weather radio.

One of the smoothest weasel moves a woman can make is to buy a new shirt for a guy. She gets the fun of shopping, she fulfills a gift-giving obligation, and she gets to look at a guy in a nicer shirt. All the guy gets is a shirt that is much lighter than a pair of binoculars or a high-performance muffler.

The hardest kind of gift to buy is a present for your boss. You want to create a false sense of respect and caring without spending any real cash. A card won't do the job. You might as well tattoo "downsize me" on your forehead.

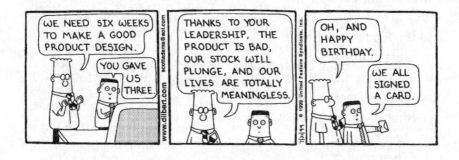

Your best bet is to buy a gift that relates to your boss's favorite hobby. If it's something easy like golf, there's no end to the crap you have to choose from. But if your boss is into fine wine or hang gliding, you're pretty much screwed as far as getting something cheap. That's why it's good to pool your money with other employees' and send the boss's secretary out to get the gift. This method is inexpensive, and if your boss doesn't like it, he'll blame his own secretary.

Dining Alone

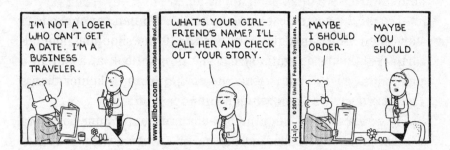

When you dine alone at a restaurant, you are providing a service to the other patrons. Everyone will enjoy staring at you and whispering about what a loser you are. They'll feel good that they aren't you, and that will release endorphins in their brains so the food tastes better.

Just kidding!

In reality the other diners are thinking what a confident and self-assured person you are to be eating all alone. They're discussing what a brilliant thinker and a generous lover you must be.

Just kidding!

They really think you're a loser. The best you can do is to try to confuse their accurate perceptions by pretending to *prefer* eating alone. The most popular method, especially for women, is to bring reading materials and never look up. If you have hair that falls forward to cover the sides of your face, use it. The scenario works best if you combine boring-looking documents, a concerned scowl, and wrinkled eyebrows. That makes you look like a powerful businessperson who is a force to be reckoned with. Not a loser.

My preferred method of solo dining is to stare straight ahead as though my brain has just dissolved. I tighten my butt muscles until it hurts so much I get a dopey look in my eyes. Then I try to imitate the *Mona Lisa*'s enigmatic smile. When I tire of that, I'll start slamming bread into my maw like it's the last food on earth. The key is to stuff each piece of bread in your mouth as soon as the prior load is going down the chute. You don't want any awkward dead time when people are watching.

The gutsiest lone-diner move is to make eye contact with the nearest table of so-called normal people and try to hijack their conversation. If they are far away, this might involve some shouting. Listen for the mention of any geographic location, product, or event that sounds familiar and then interject your own anecdote as though there's nothing unusual about you joining in. If it's a table of timid people, you can start scooting your chair closer with every sentence until your elbows are on the table. When someone gets up to use the rest room, take the empty chair and start ordering expensive wine for the table. Remember to move back to your table when it's time for the check.

Weasel Apologies

People demand apologies for practically everything these days. Apologies don't cost money, and they make people happy, so you'd think weasels would be handing them out like candy. My policy is that I'll apologize for anything bad that has happened to anyone, including in prehistoric times, parallel universes, hallucinations, acts of nature—you name it. In fact, while I'm thinking about it, I apologize to you for this book.

My only exception to the universal apology rule is those situations where I offend people on behalf of other people. For example, if I do a biting comic about, say, circus clowns, I will get a barrage of e-mail complaining about my unfair stereotyping of clowns. But *none of the mail will be from the clowns themselves.* Instead, the angry letters will come from people who are incensed that I insulted clowns who have done nothing to warrant the unfair attacks. They will invariably say something like "You wouldn't dare say something cruel about [insert name of any oppressed minority group], so what makes you think it's okay to insult clowns?"

If I'm pressed against the wall, I will resort to a weasel apology. A weasel apology sounds like a regular apology but without taking any of the blame. For example, I might say to the person who is mad about my treatment of clowns, "I'm sorry that you feel that way."

It's true, I'm genuinely sorry that anyone feels like a frickin' nut. Notice that I'm not apologizing for what I did, I'm only expressing my heartfelt sympathy for nuts. Yet it looks like an apology if you read it quickly, especially if you're expecting a real apology. Feel free to borrow this method.

Here's a report of a weasel who successfully used this technique:

Dear Mr. Adams,

A coworker filed a grievance against a supervisor because of sexist remarks and obscenities he'd shouted while criticizing her work. The coworker was waiting on customers at the time and they overheard the tirade. I witnessed the exchange so I became her support person at the grievance hearing. Management's solution was this: the supervisor had to apologize to the employee.

His apology was "I'm sorry that you made me lose my temper."

When my coworker questioned the wording of the apology, management told her that it would have to suffice unless she wanted to be "petty" and take the issue to arbitration.

Song Weasels

Sometimes when you're in your car with a weasel, and a great song comes on the radio, the weasel will start singing along. This has two benefits (for the weasel):

1. The weasel enhances his or her enjoyment of the song.

2. The weasel obliterates any hope that you will enjoy the song too.

I once made the mistake of mentioning to a song weasel during midscreech just how rude this practice is. This earned me a death stare. Apparently it's not polite to mention song-weaseling while it's happening. I still don't know why. It must be one of those unwritten rules.

Conversation Weasels

Talking is more fun than listening. That's why conversation weasels try to do all the talking and leave you with the nodding and the uh-huhs and the brain paralysis.

One excellent weasel technique for monopolizing conversation is to stop periodically to ask "Right?" about statements of obvious facts while avoiding topics that lend themselves to potential disagreement. For example, the weasel might say, "Tuba players play tubas, right?" That puts you in the position of saying something like "Um . . . yeah," which counts as your contribution to the conversation for the next ten minutes.

15

Nature Lovers

I think everyone on earth considers himself a "nature lover" without the slightest feeling of irony. The most curious members of this club are the nature lovers who like to shoot as much of nature as their ammo budget allows. They figure you can love nature just as much when it's riddled with holes. In fact, you can see a lot more of nature once you create peepholes through all the animals.

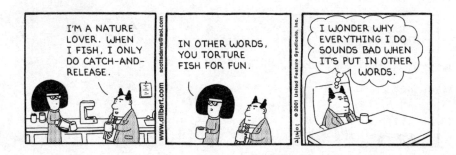

But it does beg the question of what kind of person could be called *not* a nature lover. I like to be a trailblazer, so I hereby volunteer to be the first—and probably only—nature hater.

This isn't much of a stretch for me. Recently some red squirrels ripped the shingles off a major part of my house. (Apparently they knew a huge nut was inside. Bah-dum-pum!) But seriously, folks, I was under squirrel siege for a month. Red squirrels are a protected species around here, so I had to hire a company to capture them using traps that are humane, meaning that a human would be happy to be inside one. The company promised to take the happy squirrels to a place in the mountains that is widely considered a squirrel paradise. It's in a town I had never heard of despite having lived in this area all of my adult life, but I believe it exists. Granted, it would be more cost-effective for the company to just whack the squirrels and leave them on the road so it looks like an accident. Or they could release the squirrels a block away and hope they find their way back to my house. (The company gets paid per squirrel.) But I believe their story that they drive each squirrel a hundred miles away and release it. The part I don't believe is that they give each squirrel a shampoo and a paw massage.

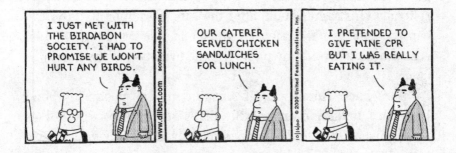

Animals Are Weasels Too

I'm writing this with a bloody face thanks to my cat Sarah, the biggest weasel in the animal kingdom. My other cat, Smokey, who is large and aggressive, likes to chase Sarah into corners and kitty-slap her until she screams. Sarah believes that the humans in the house should take some responsibility for getting rid of the bully. Her weasel method of dealing with the situation at 3 A.M. is to take a defensive position on one side of my bed and then, when chased, to escape directly across my sleeping face. This method actually works because I instantly wake up swearing, which effectively blocks Smokey's path of pursuit with my bloody skull. If Sarah could talk, I think she would say, "Hey, it's not my fault if you brought a bully in the house. I told you it was a bad idea from the start. Maybe you should sleep with a helmet."

Horses are weasels too. I recently went horseback riding at a popular mountain vacation spot. The concept, as I understood it, was to enjoy spectacular views while sitting atop one of nature's greatest creatures—the horse.

I should have been suspicious when a filthy horse-tending guy with three teeth and a cowboy hat asked a customer to relinquish his camera until after the trip. I assumed that the "no camera" rule was for safety reasons. I soon learned that the real reason was to avoid any photographic evidence of the horror to come.

Horseback riding can, I imagine, be a wonderful bond between human and animal. But that's not the case with horses that transport doughnut-fattened tourists up and down a mountain all day. This situation is more akin to humans torturing horses. But the horses have their weasel ways of getting even. It's a fair fight.

I had the bad fortune to be mounted on the last in a line of nine tired and angry horses. The majestic animals in front of me were laying down a cumulative fog of equine flatulence best described as a cross between a Mel Brooks movie and the mustard gas attacks of World War I. Luckily the trail was so dry and dusty that dirt blocked my nostrils and threatened to erase the contours of my face. By the end of the ride we had so much dust caked on our snouts that we looked like a family of light gray, noseless people with huge heads.

My horse, Tex, had a brilliant weasel technique for messing with my mind. Much of the trip was via a narrow path up a steep mountainside, where one wrong step meant certain death. Tex liked to point his head toward the cliff, as if he intended to go that way at any moment. I don't know if a horse has ever committed suicide by jumping off a cliff, but Tex had every reason to want to. His nostrils were larger than mine so even the dust of the trail couldn't fill them and protect him from the stench. I would have sworn that Tex was intentionally making his face look all worried and depressed just to scare me. If I were a depressed horse, I know I'd want to take a tourist with me.

I'm told there was scenery at the top of the mountain, but I had my eyes closed because of the dust storm and the fear of imminent cliff death. So I didn't see anything but the inside of my own eyelids.

Later that evening, as I was burning my clothes, I realized I had new respect for the pioneers who settled this great country of ours. Especially the ones who ate their horses.

16

Weasel Debating Techniques

Nothing makes a weasel argue more vigorously than being proven wrong. Here's a good example to demonstrate my point:

> Dear Mr. Adams,
>
> The department that reimburses employees in my company is infested with weasels.
>
> Recently, they refused to reimburse my boss for "Zuppa di Pesce," which he had at a dinner with an interviewee. The reasoning was that *zuppa di pesce* is wine and they don't reimburse for alcohol. *Zuppa di pesce* means "soup of fish" and is a stew of mussels, clams, and codfish with herbs, tomatoes, and garlic.
>
> Although we have sent a copy of the restaurant menu, they still will not reimburse him because "it sounds like the name of a wine."

Here are some things you'll never hear a weasel say:

I'll be darned—the information you gave me has changed my opinion. I was completely wrong.

Now that you mention it, maybe all those Nobel Prize–winning scientists *do* know more about science than I do.

I'm ignorant of the important facts so it wouldn't make any sense to offer my opinion.

The traditional method for approaching an argument is to bring up relevant facts and weave them together in a logical framework. Unfortunately, that won't work against weasels because they use a superior debating method that involves conjuring up hallucinations, carefully arranging them in a tangled lump, and declaring victory. I recommend that you use this method too because the traditional method will only leave you frustrated. The weasel techniques are detailed below using a handy abbreviation and numbering system where WDT stands for "weasel debating techniques." Feel free to use this shorthand at your next meeting, as in "Hey, Wally, are you giving me a WDT3?"

WDT 1: Restate your opponent's ideas using bizarre absolutes and then refute them, like this:

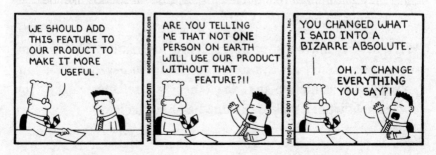

WDT 2: Make comparisons to Hitler. This is a surprisingly flexible technique because Hitler was a busy guy. He did everything from eating to painting landscapes to attacking the world. So if someone argues that napping is good for you, point out that Hitler liked napping too.

WDT 3: Make a good point about an unrelated topic. For example, if someone is arguing that airline travel is relatively safe, and you—against all data—are arguing the other side, point out that swimming is good exercise. When your opponent looks stunned and says, "Yes, but . . .," cut him off in midsentence, declare victory, and excuse yourself from the room.

WDT 4: Fill all the airtime to appear knowledgeable and eliminate the opportunity for rebuttal.

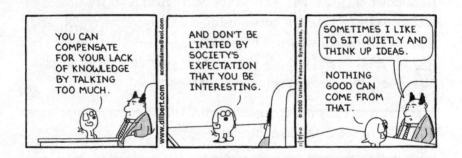

WDT 5: Accuse your opponent of being insensitive. This method works because it's always true. I'm willing to bet that even conjoined twins complain that the other is insensitive, e.g., "You don't know what it's like to be the head on the left!"

WDT 6: For every respectable human quality there is an insulting word that means the same thing. For example, accuse openminded people of being flakes. Accuse cautious people of being afraid of change, like this:

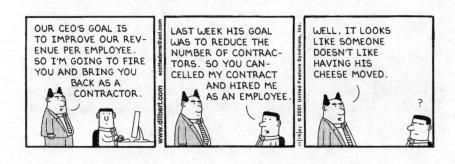

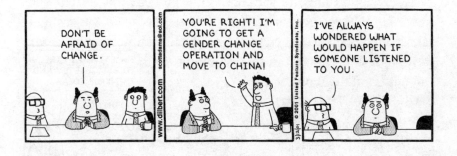

WDT 7: Add weight to your opinions by invoking the opinions of unnamed multitudes, as in "Everyone agrees with me." A weasel defines *everyone* as at least one other weasel.

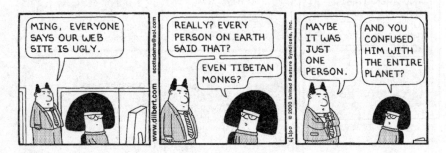

WDT 8: The tax code is a valuable debating tool for weasels because it's too complicated to understand. That means you can refer to the tax code to support any argument. I can't tell you how many times weasels have—with straight faces—suggested I invest in money-losing ventures so that I can get valuable tax write-offs. Apparently the theory is that the more money I lose the better off I will be.

Dear Mr. Adams,

A friend of mine once complained that he had been overlooked many times for promotions. People on other teams were being promoted all around him. His boss explained to him that if he were to be promoted, he would get more money, be pushed into a higher tax bracket, and thus have to pay more taxes. His boss said he wanted to save him that agony. We all started calling his boss "The Weasel."

Agreeing with Weasels

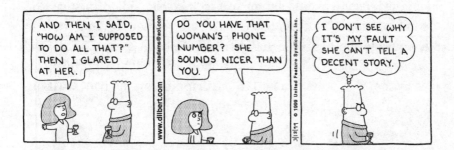

Here's something that always makes me feel awkward: I'll be listening to some weasel rant about a recent argument or injustice, hoping for sympathy, when it becomes clear to me that the weasel telling the story is 100 percent to blame and belongs in a Turkish prison. It usually goes like this:

"So we took the kids to this five-star restaurant like usual. They're both toddlers so naturally I let them shriek uncontrollably throughout the meal so they can enjoy the experience. They're screaming away, not bothering anyone—you know, just being kids—when little Todd flings a bread plate. Well, normally that would have been fine, but a guy across the room was on one knee proposing to his date and the plate hits him in the back of the head and knocks his toupee into her soup. Then little Jessica sees how much fun that was and starts throwing everything that isn't nailed down. It was so funny we were just laughing. Bob went out to the car to get his video camera. I had to borrow some things from other tables to reload Jessica so we could get some food-throwing on tape. Before long everyone starts glaring at us like we're bad parents or something just because we don't overdiscipline our children. Don't you hate people like that, Scott? Don't you? Huh?"

Obviously it would be no use to take the side of justice and common sense in this discussion. But neither do you want to encourage the behavior you just heard about. I usually take the weasel approach of asking a question like "What kind of plates were they?" It sounds as if I'm participating in the conversation, yet I'm not making any kind of commitment.

17

Whining Like a Weasel

I've noticed that people have the same need to complain no matter how good their life is. Apparently we're born with a certain amount of whining in our systems and we have to get it all out before we die.

I complained a lot when I was in my twenties, but I figured that was because I was a huge loser and had a lot to complain about. I was living alone in a one-room, four-hundred-square-foot San Francisco apartment. All of my furniture was second-hand, including my bed. I suspect that a broccoli salesman had farted into the mattress for thirty years and then died in it, only to be discovered six months later. During the daytime I put large pillows on my bed and called it a couch.

Let me tell you, nothing impresses the ladies like coming back from a date in a brown Plymouth Colt with a caved-in grill, circling the block for forty-five minutes to find parking, then getting the tour of the four-hundred-square-foot apartment. "Do you want to sit on the couch?" I'd say. "It looks like a bed, but when you prop the pillows up along the wall, it's exactly like a couch. I got it cheap because I think someone died in it. But don't worry about that. I'm sure they sprayed it. Did you know there's a guy who does nothing but clean up crime scenes? I'd hate to see his monthly bill for rubber gloves."

Luckily for me I was blessed with a bad personality so I rarely had to suffer the humiliation of showing my "home" to a date. Most nights I stayed home and watched my almost-color TV. By *almost-color*, I mean it had colors, but they weren't the ones intended by the producers of the shows. For the first two seasons of *Miami Vice* I thought Crockett and Tubbs were orange and green. And the picture rolled continuously unless I stood in one corner of the apartment to avoid absorbing the incoming TV signals.

When I was a kid in upstate New York, I had that same problem of a continuously rolling TV picture. Luckily my little Montgomery Ward's TV set had its horizontal-control knob on the side. So I wrapped a long string around the knob and tied the two ends to my feet so I could keep the picture centered from across the room. Ah, those were the days. But my San Francisco TV had the horizontal control in the back, and I didn't have the energy to rig a pulley system that would go around a corner. Instead I stood in the kitchen area, behind the TV, and watched via a mirror. That arrangement worked pretty well except that most of the people looked left-handed.

I looked forward to Saturday mornings when I would buy a newspaper and go to the little diner down the street to stare at a waitress (or "server" for the politically correct crowd) named Becky. A half dozen regulars (losers) like me usually showed up every Saturday morning for the same reason, to sit at the counter and stare at Becky. The trick was to read things near the top of the newspaper so the staring wasn't so obvious. I'd make witty conversation when the opportunity presented itself, things like "I'll have the scrambled eggs—*again!* Ha ha!" None of what I said made much sense, especially after my thirty-fifth coffee refill, but I knew this was a marathon, not a sprint. Maybe Becky wouldn't ever find me appealing, but she might get used to me, and that was progress. I just had to beat the other six losers who were using the same strategy. Occasionally some stranger who didn't understand the system would come in and actually ask her out on a date, which seemed completely unfair because he hadn't put in his time like the rest of us. But Becky usually said no, then we contestants (losers) would get our coffee refills and things would get back to normal.

The most exciting part of my life was going to work and sitting in my cubicle at the bank. I had a different job every six months, but they all had one thing in common: they weren't necessary. In those days all you needed was any kind of story to justify your job and you could keep it. You could say, "I'm analyzing the feasibility of . . ." or "I'm collecting data for . . . ," and it didn't matter how you ended the sentence—you had a job. Sometimes I had so much nothing to do that I worked overtime doing it—studying this, compiling that, reporting on whatever. My data was always deeply flawed but it didn't matter because no one used it.

The point is that when I whined about my life in those days, it all seemed appropriate. I was shocked and surprised to find that as life improved, I had exactly the same amount of complaints. And I'm not alone. This became most obvious when—thanks to *Dilbert*—I moved to a nice neighborhood where the people have plenty of money. You'd think that rich folks would complain less than the average person, but you'd be wrong. At a recent gathering I took note of the following complaints (seriously):

- The limousine service to the airport is sometimes late

- The maids bump the furniture with the vacuum cleaners

- Tennis elbow

- DSL Internet service is unreliable

I'm not exaggerating. Those were literally the problems that were burdening people.

Your first reaction might be that those seem like pretty small problems. But if those are the only problems you have, you have to make the best of them so you can get some airtime in conversations. And—let's be honest—it just feels good to complain sometimes. When you have real problems, it sounds natural. But in my neighborhood the conversations go something like this.

Neighbor 1: My maid keeps bumping the furniture with the vacuum cleaner. It's leaving dents!

Neighbor 2: I know exactly what you mean. Every piece of furniture in my house has chips in the legs.

Neighbor 1: I have a theory about the lost city of Atlantis. I don't think it experienced a natural catastrophe. I think they had maids.

Neighbor 2: Exactly. The maids kept chipping away at all the furniture with vacuum cleaners until there was nothing left but sawdust, then they vacuumed it up and the whole city was gone.

Neighbor 1: I have half a mind to do the vacuuming myself. But I have this tennis elbow.

Neighbor 2: Same here. Why is it that the maids never get tennis elbow? Do you think they play with special tennis rackets?

Promoting a Book

If your worst problems sound like luxuries to other people, you need to compensate by exaggerating. People want your stories to feature some agony and, ideally, humiliation. Couch your whining in inflated and colorful terms. I recommend including stinky animals in the narrative. I'll give you an example.

Let me whine about how it feels to promote a bestselling book in case you have the misfortune of writing one. Imagine that you are in Pamplona, Spain, during the traditional running of the bulls. You're viewing from a second-story window when suddenly you get food poisoning and vomit so violently that you propel yourself out the window and into the middle of a thousand stampeding bulls. Imagine how that would feel. Got it? Well, promoting a book isn't like that.

Now imagine that despite several broken bones you start running for your life with hundreds of angry bulls closing in fast. The bull behind you jabs your broken ribs, impales your kidney, and turns you into a human projectile, comically resulting with your head firmly wedged in the butt cheeks of the bull in front of you. Now imagine that the bull (the one who has your head) starts bucking wildly, snapping your body like a towel, liquefying your spine, while tourists videotape you and laugh, and all the other bulls gather around to wipe their noses on your body and bite you. A CNN camera crew captures the whole thing and broadcasts it to the world with the tag line, "Man Plays Cruel Prank on Animal."

Promoting a book is *almost* like that.

Now, imagine that the paramedics finally arrive, and because they hate tourists, they decide to play a prank on you. They shout to you through the bull's mouth that you need to chew your way out. And by the way, you're the president of PETA, which is having its annual convention in the hotel across the street. And all the convention attendees are on the sidewalk rooting for the bull.

Promoting a book is kind of like that, except the food isn't as good.

Authors and publishers have slightly different goals when it comes to the promotion of a book. The author, if he is ambitious, wants to put every bit of energy into promoting the book—right up to, but short of, dying from exhaustion. The publisher wants to take it a little further because nothing sells books like an author whose immortal soul leaves his body during a book signing. So you always have that awkward tension between the author trying to survive and the publisher trying to kill him.

The first step in book promotion is to convince famous people to give you insincere quotes that can be put on the back cover. The hard way to get those quotes is to write a sensational manuscript then mail it to a famous person's agent, who forwards it to the famous person's assistant, who gives it to the gardener to hold down the tarp in the back of his truck.

Fortunately, there's an easier way. Your publisher probably knows lots of famous people personally and has no shame about asking for favors. And fortunately for you, getting famous people to lie is about as hard as convincing a dog to lick himself in front of company, i.e., it's something that comes naturally and they take pride in being flexible.

Famous people have a thousand ways to say nice things about a book without actually saying anything. Here are a few book blurbs I've seen lately:

Flattering Book Quote	Real Meaning
. . . a thorough exploration!	I got the gist on page two but it went on for another three hundred.
. . . highly readable!	It has words and they are arranged in sentences.
. . . more than a book!	It can also hold down a tarp.

18

Weasels Are from Venus

I realize that everything I say about women in this section is a gross generalization, unfair, untrue, and the result of my poor perception. In other words, it's just like everything else I say. Later in the book I will say bad things about men to even up things.

That said . . .

There are two types of women: the ones who are currently in discomfort, and the ones who are actively seeking it. That's why women are more effective weasels than men—because women get some sort of bizarre enjoyment out of feeling bad.

In the first group—the women currently in discomfort—the most popular causes include childbirth, menstrual cramps, headaches, men, and wearing bad shoes.

In the second camp—the voluntary pain-seekers—we have the women who feel fine but are planning to watch sad movies, imagine bad things that don't exist, pick fights with men over things the men didn't mean to say, and shop for uncomfortable shoes.

Here's the basic difference between men and women: As a man, if I get tricked into watching a sad movie, and it's a well-crafted film, it makes me feel sad. As far as I can tell, feeling *sad* is exactly like feeling *bad*. I don't like it. If tears are shooting out of my eyes, I take that as a sure sign that I'm having a bad time. But a woman can watch a depressing movie, cry a river, and come away thinking it was a *good* time. She might even buy the book so she can feel bad again later.

Men are comfort seekers and discomfort avoiders. I think I speak for most men when I say we only enjoy pain when it happens to other people, also known as entertainment. To illustrate my point, consider these two choices for things to do on a Saturday night:

Sit on a comfortable couch and watch television while sipping delightful beverages and belching.

Or

Drive for two hours to visit people who only talk about their collection of porcelain frogs and their health problems.

A man will quite sensibly choose the couch. A woman—because women are more "social"—will choose a night of intense anguish followed by a long drive home while recapping the more dreadful points of the discussion in case the man succeeded in not listening the first time.

Women know how to inject pain into any situation. If a man has no reason to fight with a woman, she will sense the void and talk nonstop until some sort of pain is generated. For example, a man might begin to doze off or attempt to change the subject. That's proof that he doesn't care about the woman, and it's grounds for a fight.

When you combine the natural pickiness of women with

their ability to endure pain, you have a formula for total weasel domination. It begins with small corrections to men: "Don't step there," "Don't eat that," "Hand me that," and "Clean that up." Men might not agree with these little corrections, sometimes thinking they *should* step there, *should* eat that, *should* hand over something else, and *should* clean up later. But they've seen enough *Star Trek* episodes to know it's easier to obey than to get into a fight with an entity that enjoys pain.

Over time, men are trained to do what they are told so they can avoid discomfort. Show me a man who has been married for thirty years and I'll show you a man who has no opinions whatsoever.

Men Are Unacceptable

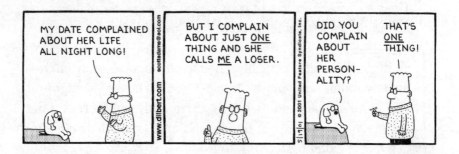

Someday historians will look back at our time and marvel how women convinced men that *socially unacceptable* means the same thing as *male*. It will be considered the greatest weasel maneuver of all time.

If you think about all the characteristics associated with men, you notice a pattern. Here's a partial list of things men do:

- Scratching groin in public
- Being too loud
- Making sexual comments
- Swearing
- Using sleeve as napkin
- Ignoring family to play golf

I could go on, but that's enough to make my point: everything that is normally identified as typical male behavior is either flat-out illegal or at least socially unacceptable. This situation evolved gradually so it snuck up on men. In the 1600s a guy could do everything on that list plus carry on a lively romance with livestock and no one would think twice. Then someone invented the napkin and it's been nothing but trouble ever since.

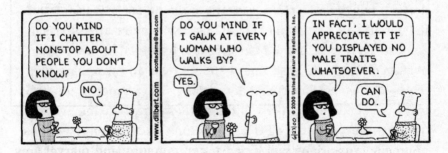

Glass Ceiling

Now I'm going to blaze a trail into politically incorrect territory, displaying a death wish even more intense than in the first part of this chapter. I begin with a thought experiment. Imagine two individuals who have identical talent and experience. They are both presented with the goal of running to the top of a mountain. The only difference between them is that one desperately wants to get to the top of the mountain (because he thinks it will help him get sex later) and the other would be happier complaining about snakes. Which of these two people is more likely to make it to the top first?

Answer: I think we can all agree that the person with the strongest incentive to get to the top of the mountain will get there first, all other things being equal.

Now consider men and women and their careers. (Here it comes.) The "correct" viewpoint is that men and women have equal talent but women are prevented from getting to the top of the corporate mountain by the "glass ceiling" of discrimination. I have to confess that the "correct" viewpoint seems a bit dodgy to me. I agree that discrimination is part of the story, but I think there's something else going on here too.

To set the stage for my elegant point, let's enjoy another wonderful analogy that's more relevant to the business world. Imagine a man and a woman of equal talent who enter an ass-kissing contest. They walk into a huge airplane hangar that has a line of overweight, middle-aged men bending over and dropping their pants to present their rumps for kissing. The winner of the contest—the one who can make it the farthest down the line without quitting—becomes the CEO of a Fortune 500 company. At this point the woman will organize a committee to talk about the glass ceiling while the man is about halfway down the line, kissing every cheek and slipping his business card in every crack. Years later a survey will show that all CEOs of major companies are men. The conclusion will be that discrimination prevented women from climbing the corporate ladder.

I blame this whole glass-ceiling problem on the practice of door-holding. Women are used to having doors held open for them by men. They get served first at restaurants, they get to leave elevators first. It's hard to move from that mind-set to kissing a huge line of asses in an airplane hangar. By contrast, men are the ones holding the doors and getting served last. For us it's not such a big step to drop and pucker, so we're more conditioned for managerial success.

I haven't met many women whose goal was to be the CEO of a Fortune 500 company. Most of the women I know prefer to be in careers that involve hanging around with people who are suffering, presumably so they can watch. For example, women are drawn to the health-care field (to watch people die), and they are well represented in law schools (to watch people get sued or executed).

You're probably racking your brain and thinking of all the exceptions to my gross generalizations. I'm sure you know several men and women who don't fit my stereotypes. But forget about your statistically irrelevant anecdotal information. Just show me the results of the following survey.

HYPOTHETICAL SURVEY QUESTION

If you could become CEO of a Fortune 500 company, and all you had to do to get there was kiss one thousand fat, white asses and never see your own children, would you do it?

If men and women answer that survey question the same way, I'll admit I'm wrong and that the glass ceiling explains everything. But I think 100 percent of women would say, "No thank you," whereas a healthy 30 percent of men would say, "Let me get my business cards out of the car."

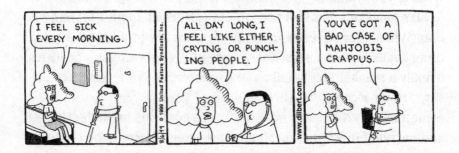

Spousal Weasels

Some weasels have learned how to turn other people into their slaves by harnessing the power of low standards. For example, if you aren't particularly bothered by sitting around in your own filth, you can manipulate your spouse or roommate into doing all the cleaning for you. If you can convince yourself it doesn't matter that corn is growing from your carpet, then you have all the power in the relationship.

Sometimes you can make your spouse do your bidding by noticing something that needs to be done and asking your spouse to do it, before your spouse notices first and asks you to do it. Whoever asks first will immediately gain moral authority over the other. No one knows why.

Women have mastered this technique to control the men in their life. But this method only works with smaller tasks. For example, if you say, "Honey, would you make the bed? I have to brush my teeth," it would seem petty for your spouse to resist the request, especially since you've offered a reason why you aren't doing it yourself. The implication is that if the roles were reversed, you would happily make the bed. In reality, being a weasel, you would be pretending you didn't hear the request.

It's good to build up gradually toward total spousal domination. When your spouse is in another room, try to think of something that's in that room that you need brought to you. There's usually a magazine or a pillow or something that you need. Then say, "Honey, could you bring me that (insert item) when you come this way?" No spouse will argue about picking up an item and carrying it a few feet in your direction. Once you have your spouse trained for simple fetching duties, expand the commands to things like "Honey, if you're going to drink the last of the milk, why don't you clean the refrigerator while you're there?"

Notice the clever method of presenting the command as a question—specifically a difficult question. As the victim of this technique you have to decide whether to get into a long *debate* on the merits of cleaning the refrigerator versus *actually* cleaning it. Both options take about the same length of time, and when you're done arguing, you'll still end up cleaning the refrigerator.

For those unpleasant and unexpected jobs around the house, you can also use the "power of not noticing" to get your spouse to handle the dirty work. For example, if you have a cat, you'll regularly find little surprises around your carpet. If you see it first, you're pretty much expected to clean it up. The trick is to avoid seeing it first and especially to avoid being nearest to it. I hate to admit just how good I have become in this method, but there's a room in my house I haven't stepped into since the Clinton presidency.

Sometimes you can convince a spouse that he or she is your remote-controlled robot. You do this by waiting until it's obvious what he is going to do in the next moment, such as wipe down a counter or put away a jar of jelly. Then you say, "Could you wipe down that counter?" or "Would you mind putting away the jelly?" Eventually your spouse will notice that everything he does is preceded by your request to do that thing. His sense of cause and effect will get confused and he'll come to believe he is a voice-activated robot with no free will.

If you're a man, you know there are two types of chores for you around the house. There are the things that you can do on your own (man's work), and then there are the things you have to help your wife do because it involves one or more of these things:

(A) Heavy objects

(B) Grotesque dead creatures

(C) Greasy and/or smelly things

(D) Mortal danger

(E) Pretending your opinion matters

So if, for example, a female spouse wants to go shopping, the male spouse will end up carrying heavy packages from the car. This arrangement seems natural and even helpful. But for some weasel reason, this helpfulness doesn't normally extend to "man's work." Sometimes a man might want to say to his spouse, "Honey, while I power-clean the gutter with this hose, you hold a bucket under the eaves and try to catch as much of the falling debris as you can before it hits our nice lawn." But because he's smart, the man will not say that. He will do his man's work without grumbling, until such time as he writes a book about weasels.

19

Weasel Products

Have you noticed all the great products on the market lately? For example, I keep hearing radio ads for a product that grows hair on bald guys. I'm not talking about the famous products that temporarily make a little bit of "cosmetically acceptable" hair grow back on some people sometimes if they use it every day. Apparently, with this new product you can just pour it over your head and yell, "Stand back!"

The amazing thing about this hair growth product is that it's not the biggest story in the entire world. This is puzzling to me. For some reason the company needs to advertise on the radio instead of taking advantage of the worldwide pandemonium that an effective hair-growing formula is sure to make. They really need to get a new PR person.

Another great product is a pill you take and then lose weight without doing anything special. That company does a lot of advertising too. They must be using the same ineffective PR agency as the hair growth people. You would think that in a country where 60 percent of the population can't use a bicycle for fear of crushing it, a highly effective weight-loss pill would create a buzz on its own. I'll bet the newspapers would do stories on this great product if they only knew it existed. Apparently newspaper people don't listen to the radio.

My favorite new product is a gadget you attach to your stomach to build abdominal muscles while you sit in a chair watching television. This is an excellent first step, but I want similar products for the rest of my body too. My dream is to cover myself with electrodes, go to sleep at night, and wake up looking like the Incredible Hulk, but without the attitude.

And again, the news media seems to have missed a major story here, about how exercise is no longer necessary. I suppose that individually these great products aren't interesting enough for front-page news. But I'm planning to use them all in conjunction. I'll be sprouting hair, losing weight, and growing huge muscles without ever leaving my couch. I might even learn Spanish while I'm asleep.

For a while I was hearing lots of ads for a natural herb that makes your brain work better. I don't hear those ads anymore. Maybe the makers of the hair growth products, weight loss pills, and abdominal exercise devices didn't want people to do a better job of thinking. It's probably bad for business.

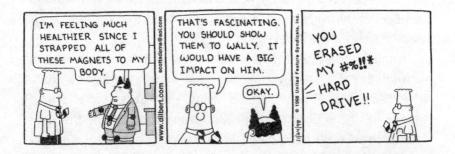

For the record, so no one sues me, I have not seen the scientific studies supporting any of these products, but *I totally believe those studies exist.*

Planned Weaselescence

I like to complain about defective products, but I understand that the economy would collapse if people could, for example, buy a lightbulb that lasts a thousand years or a computer that really is upgradeable.

Most houses are built out of wood and we've come to accept that as a logical choice. Wood was a major innovation compared to prior building concepts such as the mud hut and the hole scratched with fingernails into the side of a large tree. But in this era of plastic and steel and exotic composite materials that last forever, I couldn't understand why my house was made of termite food. Until I read this e-mail:

> Dear Mr. Adams,
>
> I work for a publisher who is concerned that our books never wear out so no one ever needs to replace them. He wants "the books to explode like you see in *Mission: Impossible*." Below is another quote from his memo to his own supervisor concerning this idea:
>
> "We are concerned that the current book is so durable that it lasts for years and negatively impacts new sales. We are going to test reducing the amount of glue in the binding so that the book will literally fall apart after one year. A book in pieces should encourage users to purchase a new copy rather than use an old one."

Antiweasel Techniques

As already mentioned, most of the products you buy at the store turn out to be defective. People tend to overlook minor defects because life is too short to fight every battle. But if the defect is huge, and the item is costly, most people will return it to the store and ask for a refund. Not me. I toss the product in the garbage, along with most of the other things I bought during the week, and mutter to myself, "Well, I should have seen that coming." I can't decide if that means I'm lazy or stupid, and frankly it's not the sort of question I like to dwell on.

At the other end of the spectrum is a person I will call Weaselgirl to protect her secret identity. Weaselgirl uses her own brand of superpowers to fight tirelessly against the weasel practices of businesses. Her method of approaching shoddy products and services could not be further from my own. Here is a handy comparison of our contrasting approaches to bad products and services.

Problem	My Solution	Weaselgirl's Solution
Service at hotel is bad.	Suffer.	Complain to manager and get 50 percent discount.
You don't know which painting will look good in your house.	Buy wrong painting and hate it every day.	Buy twelve paintings and return eleven two days later. Return the twelfth next year and claim it was defective. Repeat.
You accidentally order wrong item.	Pay for wrong item. Then buy right item.	Blame store for shipping wrong item. Demand to keep it for free. Later exchange wrong item for correct item.
You find bug in your glass of wine.	Drink wine and comment on the sterilizing effects of alcohol.	Call manager over and get the entire meal for free.
You do *not* find bug in your glass of wine.	Drink wine.	Add bug.

A while back I had a problem with my Internet provider. Their service would regularly be down for days at a time. Usually I couldn't even get them to admit it was broken. Their tech support people would make me reboot my machine seven times, reconfigure my software, and plug and unplug things. On each occasion, at the end of the hour-long process, they would finally confess that their service hadn't been working for days in my area. It seemed to me that they were having entirely too much fun spending my money and jerking me around. So I decided to take a page from Weaselgirl's book and turn up the heat on them. I figured I would demand a refund or a discount of some sort as a way of getting their attention.

But I'm not very good at this sort of thing.

After finally figuring out whom to call (they don't make it easy) and then finally getting a human (arguably) on the line, I stated my case and asked for a refund. What follows is one of the best antiweasel maneuvers ever.

The representative said she wasn't authorized to give a refund. So I demanded to speak with someone who was. The representative told me she wasn't authorized to contact anyone who had that sort of power.

I could have canceled the service, but they were the only company offering high-speed Internet service in my area, and I clung to hope that it might someday heal on its own. So the way we left it is that I would pay exorbitant fees every month and they would sometimes offer service.

20

Weasel Types

In this chapter I will explore some of the more interesting weasel types.

Oops Weasel

An Oops Weasel creates situations in which something is likely to go wrong, and when it does, the Oops Weasel benefits. It's a powerful technique in the workplace because so many things go wrong naturally that no one will notice a few extra.

For example, if an Oops Weasel wants to avoid a meeting, he'll suggest inviting a coworker who's notoriously busy. That will create a scheduling challenge for the meeting organizer and push the meeting several weeks into the future. With that much time until the meeting, the key attendees will probably have personal emergencies, illnesses, or emergency out-of-town trips that will force the meeting to be pushed back further. As a backup plan, the Oops Weasel will volunteer to reserve the meeting room and then forget to do it.

Call centers are breeding grounds for Oops Weasels. They're full of people who "accidentally" disconnect your phone after you ask a difficult and time-consuming question. Call Center Weasels get paid based on how quickly they can get rid of pesky callers.

At the first whiff of a difficult call, they'll forward you to the wrong person or put you on infinite hold until you give up. That's why call center employees don't give their real names. They're afraid that customers will hunt them down.

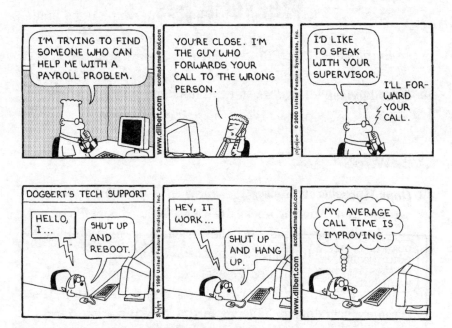

If your manager seems remarkably bad at anticipating problems, it's probably because he's an idiot. But he might also be a clever Oops Weasel *pretending* to be an idiot. Managers know that if their employees sense any sort of trouble brewing, they become like locusts, continually swarming around with questions. An Oops Weasel manager will cleverly respond by denying that any problems are likely to happen—despite all obvious signs to the contrary—and later freely confess that he was wrong, like this:

Employee: I heard that our profits are being restated lower by two billion dollars. Should I be worried about my 401K?

Oops Weasel: No, you should double your contributions. There's never been a better time to be inadequately diversified.

Employee: The FBI took away our senior management in shackles. Is that a problem?

Oops Weasel: I don't see how that can be bad. But if I'm wrong I'll be the first one to admit it.

One week later . . .

Oops Weasel: Wow, that snuck up on me.

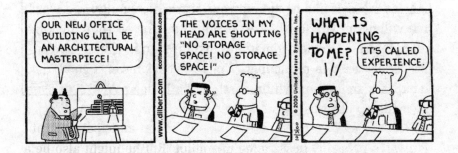

Lazy Weasel

Two popular methods for making money include:

1. Work

2. Management

Management is similar to work except that other people do the work while you make them feel bad about their performance. And if that gets too hard, you can hire a supervisor to criticize the employees for you.

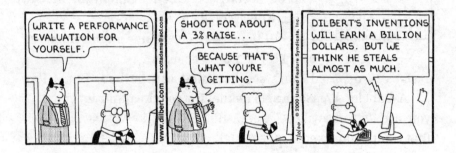

Labeler Weasel

Labeler Weasels like to sum up your entire personality in a word that will haunt you for the rest of your life. The secret to making a label stick is to pick something insulting and wrap it in wittiness so it's easy to remember. That's why it's never a good idea to express an opinion within earshot of a Labeler Weasel. It usually ends up like this:

You:	I saw a good movie on TV last night.
Labeler Weasel:	You're a couch potato.
You:	What? It's the first time I've watched TV in six years!
Labeler Weasel:	What was the movie, *Sofa's Choice*?
You:	Gaaa!! Stop being witty! Whatever you say next will be my label for life!!
Labeler Weasel:	Settle down, Spud.

A Labeler Weasel might try to trick you into bragging that you are "strong-willed." You'll think that's an admirable trait that can't be mocked. Later, with the help of the Labeler Weasel's powers of clarification, you'll realize that *strong-willed* means exactly the same as *asshole*. Armed with your confession, the Labeler Weasel will give you a witty nickname that sounds vaguely like your real name. If you're lucky, your name won't be something like Hugh Jassole.

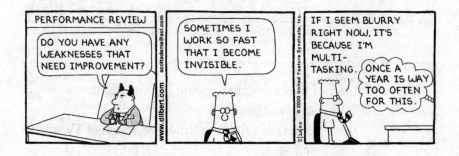

Trapper Weasel

A Trapper Weasel creates no-win situations for his victims. Managers are expert Trapper Weasels, routinely pairing employee objectives with offsetting impossibilities, like these:

- Increase sales *and* lower marketing expenses

- Focus on priorities *and* get everything done

- Stop complaining about your salary *and* don't steal office supplies

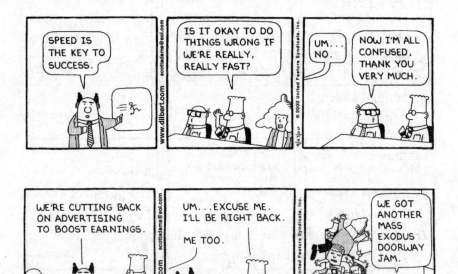

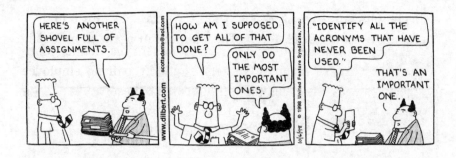

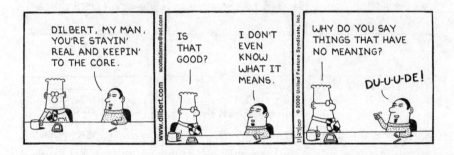

The simplest form of weasel trap is to ask someone to select from two bad alternatives and then to criticize the choice. For example:

Trapper Weasel: Should we buy or lease the equipment?

Victim: Um . . . I think we should buy it.

Trapper Weasel: Are you crazy? We don't have any money in the capital budget!

Victim: Oh . . . then we should lease it.

Trapper Weasel: That's insane! There's a corporate ban on leasing equipment!

The ultimate weasel trap is when a woman asks for a man's opinion. We always fall for it. The moment of realization looks like this:

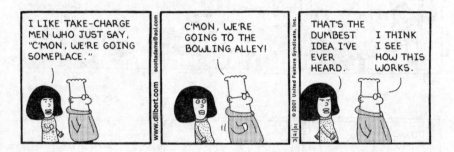

Rationalizing Weasel

A Rationalizing Weasel believes that the people around him enjoy the pollution caused by his personality. If he plays polka music in his cubicle, he believes his office neighbors are humming along. He imagines that someday they will buy him a greeting card that says, "Thanks for all the great polka music!" When he talks too loudly, it's not because he can't be quieter, it's because he believes everyone would like to hear what he has to say. If he smokes a cigar, he believes you enjoy the smoke as much as he does. In fact, you're getting a better deal than he is because you didn't pay for the cigar and the crud in his lungs has seasoned the smoke.

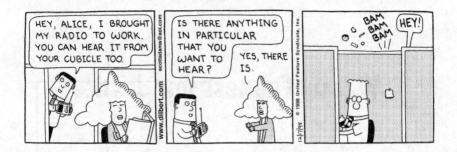

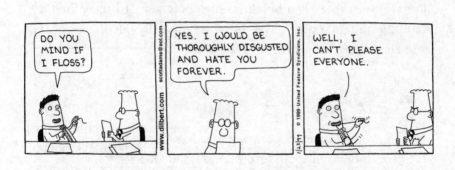

21

Weasel Fairness and Justice

For weasels, there is a big difference between ordinary theft and "setting things right." The latter is morally justified because you're making the world a better place.

Dear Mr. Adams,

The women in my department take turns providing nice brands of hand soap, tissues, and hand lotion in the ladies' room because the stuff provided by the company is miserable.

I was in the ladies' room one day when a woman from another department finished drying her hands, opened her purse, inserted the hand lotion and the soap dispenser, and tidily closed it.

When I seemed surprised, she said, "This place can afford it." I mentioned that we all took turns buying the items, and she nodded and said, "Well, I'm sure they make more money than I do, so they can afford it." She then left the ladies' room triumphantly and, I am sure, morally sure of the rightness of her actions.

The Honor System

The least effective system ever invented is something called the honor system. The theory guiding this system is that people are not huge weasels.

If there are infinite universes, as some scientists suggest, then one of those universes might have no weasels. In that universe the honor system would work like a charm. But in this universe—the weaselverse—the honor system works something like this:

Dear Mr. Adams,

I set up a little retail shop at my desk at work where I sell candy, oatmeal, and Cup-o-Noodles. It operates on the honor system. People take an item and throw the appropriate money into a tin coffee can. I've noticed that when I'm in the office and watching, this system works well. But when I'm gone, my coworkers just steal the items.

One weasel comes by regularly, takes an item, and drops what sounds like two quarters into the can. Upon closer inspection, it turns out to be two pennies or two nickels.

As if that weren't enough, sometimes when I am making copies in the room directly across from my desk, I see people walk by, take an item, and tap the can with their fingers to move around the change already in the can. This simulates the "jingling" sound of coins dropping on coins. The bastards!!!

Weasel Embezzlement

If you have the sort of job that involves sitting in a cubicle and being ignored by your boss, then you have the perfect opportunity for weasel embezzlement. Don't confuse weasel embezzlement with its highly illegal cousin "ordinary embezzlement." Weasel embezzlement isn't a crime yet, and thanks to that loophole, many weasels are enjoying the benefits. It works like this:

The key to weasel embezzlement is to get a cubicle that's away from the people who would understand what's on your screen. If you're a computer programmer, you want a cubicle in the marketing department. When the marketing people see computer code on your screen, they'll assume it has something to do with your job at the company. And when you show up for work in a Ferrari they'll assume it's because you're just like them, i.e., don't understand that *loan* means you have to give back the money.

Avoid using the phone in your cubicle to work on your second job. That's a dead giveaway. Use your personal cell phone instead, preferably while briskly walking, so no one hears more than a few words of your conversation. They'll only hear snippets out of context, like this:

Snippet 1: "... My coworkers ..."
Snippet 2: "... have no idea ..."
Snippet 3: "... what a huge flaming ..."
Snippet 4: "... weasel ..."
Snippet 5: "... I am ..."

And don't use your company e-mail account for the second job because that can easily be tracked. Get a free e-mail account on Hotmail or Yahoo!—also known as "your accomplices"—so you don't leave a trail.

I wonder who holds the world's record for secretly doing the most simultaneous jobs. I know lots of people who secretly work two full-time jobs from one cubicle. My guess is that somewhere there's a computer programmer who works at a top-secret government facility and holds the record at four simultaneous jobs:

1. His primary job as a computer programmer

2. His secret freelance programming job

3. Selling Amway products from the cubicle

4. Spying for China

The only downside, other than the extra work, is that you can't brag about your accomplishment without being fired or executed. But if you tell me, I won't tell anyone. If you have a four-jobber or better, let me know at scottadams@aol.com. I promise to be impressed.

Jury Duty

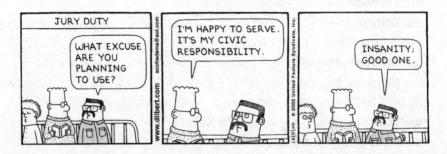

I have a theory about why our prisons are so full. I blame jury duty. Follow me on this . . .

It's relatively easy to get out of jury duty. Therefore the only people who serve on juries are people who have nothing better to do. Many of those people have jobs, which means *jury duty is more pleasant than their jobs!* Needless to say, jurors are seriously disgruntled people. If my job were less pleasant than jury duty, I'd want to convict innocent people just to see their eyes bulge when they hear the verdict. I'd want to do anything just to feel alive for a minute.

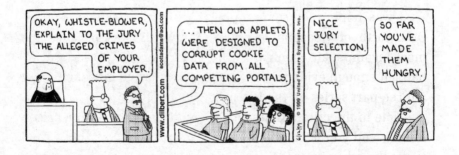

As you know, important celebrities can easily get out of jury duty. I recently discovered that cartoonists are not important celebrities. (I should really have had a backup excuse.) In my capacity as "juror eight" I sat in judgment of a guy who had committed approximately the same crimes as most of the people in the jury box, but he wasn't smart enough to get away with them. In fact, he was a three-time offender by the time we got him. So we were, in effect, deciding whether he should go to prison for life—not so much for being a criminal, but for being a dumb one that got caught. Three times.

As a responsible member of the community, and an accomplished weasel, my deliberations followed this line of reasoning:

1. The defendant owned many scary guns.

2. Good Lord, I think he might recognize me.

3. I wonder if he holds a grudge.

4. What are the odds he could break out of prison?

5. I think he keeps looking at me. *Gaaaa!!!*

I was hoping for some ambiguity in the evidence, even an O.J. worth of weasonable doubt. Sadly this was perhaps the most incompetent criminal in the history of the world, and he had left enough evidence to create his own crime museum, if not a three-part series on the Discovery Channel.

Note to the criminal: If you happen to read this in the prison library, and you later break out, I want you to know that I tried to get the other jurors to acquit you. But after twenty minutes of deliberations I got hungry and decided to send you to prison for the rest of your life so I could go get a Snickers. I hope you understand. If not, all I ask is that you whack the jurors in reverse alphabetical order.

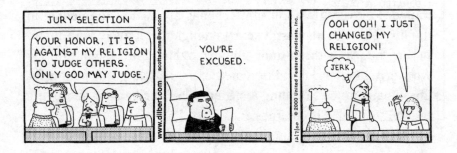

Donating Like a Billionaire

Someday you might be a billionaire. You'll be pressured to donate huge amounts of money to people who have diseases. That's a direct challenge to your goal of keeping every penny you already have and taking everyone else's money too. It's also a publicity dilemma. You want to appear generous while maintaining the egomaniacal greed that got you the money in the first place. That won't be easy because everyone you know will think it's "fair" for you to give away most of your money under the theory that it's not *their* money and someday they might get a disease.

The solution is "donating like a billionaire." Hold a press event and announce that you will be donating a billion dollars to some sort of charity, spread out over an unspecified time. You will be hailed as a generous visionary. After the hoopla dies down, you can specify the period of time over which your billion dollars will be spread. I recommend a billion years. If you're seventy years old, you'll only be out about ten bucks before you die. And these days you can't buy that kind of international goodwill for ten bucks.

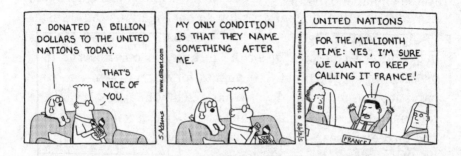

The Nigerian E-Mail Scam

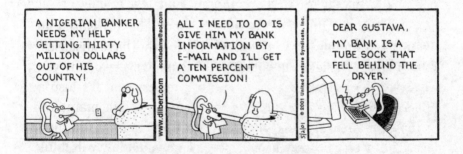

As you probably learned in high school, the entire GNP of Nigeria is based on revenue generated from e-mail scams. I get about five Nigerian scam e-mails every day. Watch this: I will check my e-mail right now and see if there is a Nigerian scam in the latest batch. Hold on . . .

Okay, I'm back. I got one scam e-mail from Zimbabwe and one from Nigeria (really). But I suspect that the Zimbabwe scam is really a Nigerian scam in disguise.

The way the Nigerian scam works is that there's allegedly a huge pile of money caught in a political or bureaucratic tangle in Nigeria. The only way to get it out is if a friendly foreigner (you) provides your banking information so the Nigerians can transfer the funds out of Nigeria and into your bank. In return for this help you get a percentage of the fortune. In other words they promise you'll get about $10 million for letting them use your bank account for a few days. What actually happens is that the Nigerians find out enough about your bank account to drain it and then disappear. They are funny that way.

But that's not the funniest part.

The funniest part is that so many people fall for it. I talked with a security director for a huge corporation who said a number of the managers at his company had lost money on this scam. These are the same managers who make billion-dollar decisions affecting the economy of the world. Here's the actual e-mail I got today, reproduced exactly. Would you fall for this?

To: scottadams@aol.com

ATTEN:PRESIDENT/CEO.

I am Engr.BOLA JOHNSON, of the Nigeria National Petroleum Corporation. I was the chairman of project Award Committee. Some years ago my corporation Awarded contract to Italian firm to supply & construction of pipeline in my ministry (NNPC) the contract was executed and the contractors were Duly paid. We now have an over-inflated bill to the tune of U.S. $38.5m Lodges with one of the First Afri Bank LTD in overseas.

After several discussions with the Accountant General of

the Federation, We found out that, this fund was still in the First Afri Bank LTD in oversea. But for the fact that we are civil servant we are not allow to operate a foreign account. Hence my colleagues and I now decided to seek your assistance by clearing the fund from the First Afri Bank LTD. We have agreed to share the fund as follow:

30% for you as the beneficiary of the fund.

60% for my colleagues and I.

10% for expenses.

However, to places you in a better position of having a claim to the said fund, we need the following from you to enable us prepare the necessary documents that will give a legal backing to the fund.

{1} YOUR PERSONAL NAME AND ADRESS OR YOUR COMPANY NAME AND ADRESS.

{2} YOUR PRIVATE TELEPHONE AND FAX NUMBERS.

Finally we have already made a proper arrangement on how you will receive the fund and all the documentation has been put in place. Be assured that, this transaction is 100% risk free. Also this transaction we needs your maximum confidentiality and trust. If you are interested in doing this business with us, kindly send me email immediately for more details.

Your response will be highly appreciated.

Thanks and remain bless.

BOLA JOHNSON

22

Miscellaneous Weasels

Consumer Weasels

You might have heard a famous story about a guy who went to Nordstrom to return a set of tires. According to the tale, Nordstrom cheerfully accepted the tires—despite that they don't sell tires—and gave the guy a refund. If you wondered whether the story is true or just an urban legend, I can settle if for you now. The day after it happened, I went to Nordstrom and bought the tires that guy returned. I intended to buy pants, but I'm afraid of shopping so I usually panic and buy whatever is sitting out by the Dumpster.

Anyway, management consultants tell the Nordstrom tire story as an example of great customer service. The consultants don't mention what happens if you're dumb enough to give great service: weasels come out of the woodwork. Weasels are irresistibly drawn to stores that have liberal return policies. To weasels, that's the same as "free." Sometimes a weasel will buy an expensive dress for a big event and return it a few days later stained with wedding cake, champagne, and DNA from the best man.*

*The DNA is from a lock of the best man's hair. If you had a different idea, you've been watching too much CNN.

Weasels never feel guilty about returning merchandise because they always have a good excuse, such as "I only needed it for one day and they were charging me like I was going to wear it for the rest of my life."

Tourist Weasels

I know a cheap weasel who enjoys traveling and collecting souvenirs. But he doesn't enjoy the part where he has to give his money to other people. He's too cowardly to be a thief so his options are limited. His weasel solution is to collect business cards everywhere he goes—hotels, restaurants, gift shops—and organize them into a binder, which I assume was stolen from work. He'll walk into a gift shop and without a shred of guilt ask the proprietor for a business card. No one ever refuses to give out a business card. Cost: zero. It is brilliant.

You can argue that a business card from a gift shop is not as good as, say, a snow globe of the Eiffel Tower. But when you stuff them both in a drawer for thirty years, it's really about the same.

Techno-Weasels

Did you ever wonder what would happen if Superman were a weasel? If he were human instead of a morally superior Kryptonian, I think it's safe to say he would be the biggest weasel ever. I mean, come on, why would a bulletproof guy ever pay for anything at 7-Eleven? Maybe I'm projecting my own personality here, but I think I speak for many of you when I say it would be fun to see a convenience-store clerk empty his handgun into my chest while I calmly ate a Snickers. The look on his face would be precious. And then he'd realize I was Superman and we would both have a good laugh. I'd probably give him a twirling superwedgie, then fly around the world real fast until I had traveled back in time and bought a winning lottery ticket. I would be called the Man of Stealing Things, if you catch my drift. Power corrupts but superpower corrupts way better. And that leads me to my topic: techno-weasels.

Techno-weasel: A weasel who knows a lot about technology.

Technical knowledge is like a superpower, albeit a weak one. It's one step below being able to make things freeze by blowing on them. Still, it's no surprise that people who have lots of technical knowledge are total weasels. You would be too if you had a superpower.

Imagine the thrill of going into a meeting and pooh-poohing every idea because it "wouldn't work" and then giving highly technical reasons that no one understands, many of them totally fabricated. The acronyms would be bouncing off your chest while you smiled and ate a breakfast pastry.

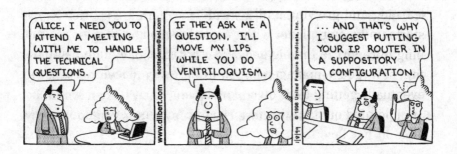

A techno-weasel's happiness is directly related to the gap between his knowledge and his boss's knowledge. The bigger the gap, the more corrupt (i.e., happy) the techno-weasel is. The perfect boss for a techno-weasel is someone who thinks a server farm is where cash cows come from. In short, you want this guy . . .

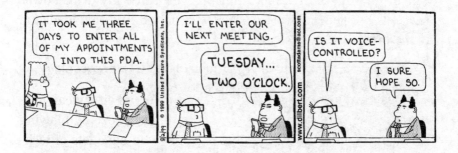

Pyramid Power

If weasels had a temple it would be shaped like a pyramid. Nothing makes people get prickly faster than pointing out that they have been duped into a pyramid scheme. That's why I like to point it out whenever possible. It's surprising how often it applies.

Recently I had a long conversation with a woman who was nice enough to explain her nonmainstream religion to me. The central belief of this religion is that every human soul continues learning and growing until it becomes a god. Then the new god starts up its own planet with people reporting to it while continuing to report to the big god who created it. The humans under the new god's management will someday become gods too, eventually getting their own planets, and so on.

I pointed out that this is a pyramid scheme. I could tell by the look on her face that *pyramid scheme* is a bad choice of words for characterizing someone else's belief system. In case you're wondering, some other words to avoid in this sort of conversation are *caper, ploy, conspiracy,* and *hatched.*

But most pyramid schemes are in the business world and look like this one:

Dear Mr. Adams,

There's a so-called marketing organization that cons people into thinking that they are applying for a job selling financial products. But before they can earn money, they have to go through a training course that costs up to $750.

Any sales they make during this training period (which they try to stretch out as long as possible) yield no income to the trainee; the trainer gets to keep all the money.

They use high-pressure techniques to suck people in, then they try to take as much money away from those people as possible. That encourages people to stay to recoup the money they've spent.

Although they deny that their company runs a pyramid scheme, it's run in the spirit of one: the people at the top get a cut of the commissions from everyone below them, and the only way to make money yourself is to "recruit" people to work under you.

I don't know how pyramid schemes got such a bad reputation. I would think that convincing people to give you money while doing little or nothing in return would be the very definition of being a winner. Capitalism has so many gray areas.

Leaders

Leaders are people you should try to avoid at all costs. As I often say, the whole point of "leading" is making you do things you didn't want to do on your own. Leaders have taken the practice of weaselness to its highest level.

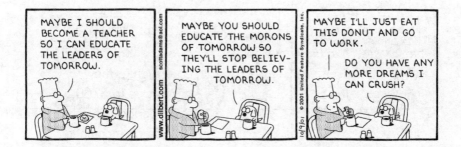

Leadership is only possible because people are, on the whole, spectacularly gullible. If you indoctrinate a human being early in life, say in grade school, you can fill its brain with virtually anything and those delusions will stay there forever. If that kid lives in your country (whatever that might be), its brain is filled with patriotism, goodness, and the right religion. If the kid is born in any other country (no matter which one), its brain is filled with hate and belligerence and a strange cultlike religion.*

*The people in those other countries see it differently. They think the delusions are on *your* end. That just goes to show how thoroughly brainwashed those crazy foreigners are. Ha ha!

Weasel Science

Science is a lot of work and that's reason enough to avoid doing it. But another good reason is that controlled, double-blind tests would eliminate some of the most popular weasel tools available.

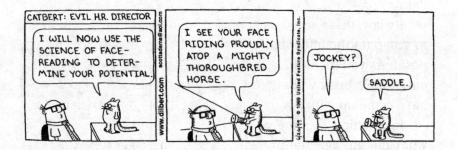

Weasel science is an improvement over actual science because it's not so limited by facts. Companies are increasingly turning to weasel science to help make important personnel decisions. They're checking handwriting, using polygraphs, and even doing face reading. But by far, the most popular weasel science is the Myers-Briggs personality types test.

The idea is that people can be categorized by personality type and you can work with them better if you take that into account. Okay, I buy that. My quibble with the theory is that if you aren't bright enough to know that people have different personalities, you're asking a lot of the Myers-Briggs training to get you over the hump. My second quibble is that their personality categories don't include weasel, moron, or flaming butt-hole. I don't know about you, but I rarely have problems with any other type of personality.

Dog-Walking Weasels

I work at home in a neighborhood where people like to walk their dogs. When I say "walk their dogs," that is a euphemism for delivering the loggified contents of the dog's intestines to the lawn of unsuspecting neighbors. I receive several deliveries a day.

By law, these serial poopers are supposed to carry a little bag to scoop up the offending deposits and carry them home for disposal. As you might imagine, this takes much of the joie de vivre out of their brisk walk in the cool morning air. The local weasels have come up with several work-arounds for this problem.

In practice, the dog walkers in my neighborhood usually do what the guy outside my window is doing right now (literally). He stands lookout while the dog defiles my flowerbed. If he sees someone watching, he will produce the little bag and do his duty on the doody. But if no one seems to be watching, he will yank the dog's leash as soon as it stops grimacing, then the two will walk briskly in the direction of a getaway. Yup, there he goes, right on cue. Weasel dog-walking bastard.

The authorities tend to go easy on this sort of crime, probably because a cute animal is involved. But if you imagine that the dog is essentially a container for delivering feces to a neighbor's lawn, I think you'll agree that it shouldn't matter how cute the container is. Imagine that the roles were reversed and your dog was walking you. I think if you looked out your window every day and found a two-hundred-pound neighbor grunting in your petunias, you would be contacting your authorities right away.

But cute dogs get away with anything. I see no logical limit to how much weasels can abuse the cute-dog loophole. Someone

should invent a cute robotic dog that doubles as a trash com-
pactor. You throw your garbage in the robot dog's mouth and
crank its tail to compact it. Then you take the dog for a "walk"
and have it deliver the semicomposted debris to the lawns of
your neighbors. If anyone sees you, just take out a plastic bag
and scoop the garbage back in, feed it to your mechanical dog,
and go searching for an unattended lawn. Over a lifetime you
could save massive amounts on garbage pickup service.

Weasel Geniuses

I'm an expert at appearing smarter than I am. I have a natural
advantage because I'm nearsighted. Glasses add ten points to
your perceived IQ. I'm also unattractive and have a boring personality, so people figure I must be good at math. And of course I
write books for a living, and that seems automatically smartish.
People don't realize that until a copy editor straightens it all out,
it looks like a dictionary for the African clicking language.

Another thing I do to appear smart is learn one or two things
about lots of different brainy subjects so I can drop tidbits into
conversations. Here are some of the ones I like to use. Feel free
to borrow them.

SMART-SOUNDING EXAMPLES

That reminds me of the Schrödinger's cat thought experiment.

Muslims call it a hajj.

Fuel cells produce drinkable water as the exhaust.

I'm thinking of becoming a fake wine expert to round out my fake knowledge. According to my friends who are either wine experts or fake wine experts—I can't tell—it's easy to act knowledgeable about wine. All you need to do is learn a lot about a few kinds of wine and always steer the conversation in that direction. If anyone mentions any other kind of wine, just say it's in your wine cellar and you're waiting for the right occasion to try it. If someone wants to see your wine cellar, say you would be happy to give a tour, but unfortunately the wine gets tannic if the door is continually opened and closed. It is not important that you know what *tannic* means.

When presented with a new wine, act as though it is the only wine on earth that you haven't tried. Get all wide-eyed and hold up the bottle to study the label while adding it to your vast mental database that includes three other labels that have all run together in your head. Use ambiguous language like "I haven't tried this vintage." That leaves open the possibility that you've tasted every other vintage. When tasting the wine, I like to do a spit-take and spray the other guests in the room while cursing in French. Then I say something like "This is the most foul thing I have had in my mouth since that one night as a Boy Scout!"

Okay, I don't really do that. But if you decide to try it, let me know how it goes.

If you plan to be a fake expert in literary matters—which incidentally goes well with fake expertise in wine—you'll have to sprinkle these words and phrases into your conversation:

zeitgeist

fin de siècle

deus ex machina

über

au courant

the third act

sine qua non

shibboleth

ex nihilo

Anything foreign, especially Latin or French or German, will sound smarter than English. I was just reading a book called *Fooled by Randomness* in which the author, Nassim Nicholas Taleb (a very smart-sounding name), made a point by using this quote along with its translation:

Aut tace aut loquere meliora silencio (only when the words outperform silence).

The author used two languages, twelve words, and two parentheses to say, "Don't be wordy." And yet it sounds quite smartish because one of the languages is foreign and was probably uttered by someone who lived a long time ago and believed you could cure leprosy by eating clay.

Here from my e-mail are some more excellent tips for appearing smart.

Dear Mr. Adams,

Based on my experiences as a software engineer, I came up with a list of five things you must do in order to be perceived as a genius in the tech industry:

(1) Be arrogant: nothing makes you look smarter than dismissing other people's ideas with utter disdain.

(2) Refuse to document anything: this guarantees that people will always have to beg you for information.

(3) Be opinionated: don't explain why you have your opinions, just put them out there and mock anyone who disagrees.

(4) Hang around with the smart people: you'll look smart if you hang around with smart people.

(5) Resist using any "process": processes are for losers. Act like you're too smart to need a process because everything you do works on the first try.

Historian Weasels

When people make up stories about the past, that's called history. History is taught in schools and is good to know because the people who do not study history are doomed to repeat the things that appear in history books but never actually happened.

It's often noted that the best part about winning a war is that you've already killed most of the people who disagree with your interpretation of events. Then you can make history books any way you want without a bunch of complaining. I assume that everything I read in history books is made up because the alleged noble motives of the heroes never pass the sniff test. For example, if you tell me George Washington turned down the chance to be king (for all practical purposes) because he loved democracy and loved his country, my weasel alarm goes off. But if you tell me he turned down another term as president so he could go back to Mount Vernon and hump his slaves without the secretary of state walking in on him every five minutes—*that* I can believe.

Soon after I wrote the first draft of this chapter, some famous historians started taking heat in the media for not having well-documented sources (i.e., for making stuff up) and for plagiarism (i.e., copying the stuff that other historians made up). These allegations came as a big shock to everyone but me. The great thing about assuming everyone is a weasel is that I'm never disappointed.

I don't blame historians for making stuff up. No one knows what happened more than a hundred years ago. In the old days, the people who wrote things down would get whacked if they offended anyone important, and it's the important people who were doing all the history-making. I would be amazed if the so-called historians got *anything* right, especially the little details.

For example, there's a big brouhaha about whether Shakespeare wrote Shakespeare's plays. If the historians can't agree on something that simple, I don't have a lot of confidence that they can explain, for example, the interplay of geopolitical and economic forces during the time of Napoleon's rule.

The latest revised historical "fact" about Napoleon is that he was actually fairly tall compared to people of his day. If Napoleon can go from being the most famous short person in history—even having a complex named after him—to "actually tall," you're probably thinking the same thing I am: Napoleon wrote Shakespeare's plays.

Fitness Weasels

I subscribe to a fitness-oriented magazine that is packed full of articles on the right way to eat and exercise. That's all they write about—eating and exercising. You might think that after the first few issues they would have said everything that needs to be said on those topics. But you'd be wrong. Amazingly, the magazine discovers new and better ways to eat and exercise *every single month!*

If you don't subscribe to any fitness magazines, you're probably using an old technique—perhaps as much as a month old—for growing huge abdominal muscles. I pity you for your ignorance and lack of results.

Thanks to my magazine subscription I learn a new and better method for growing huge abdominal muscles every thirty days. (We hardbodies like to call them abs.) At first I was skeptical that there could be so many different ways to exercise a particular muscle. It seemed to me that the experts would have figured out the one best way a long time ago. But I believe that the new methods are indeed better than the old ones because the models on the cover of the magazine have excellent abs. I assume that the models get to read the articles before we do so they can use the secrets to get in shape for the photo shoot.

I worry that with all the effectiveness of these new exercise techniques my abs might start jutting out in an embarrassing low-hanging-man-breast kind of way. That could never happen with the old methods of exercise—say six months ago—but it's a definite risk now with these new and improved methods. That's why I try to take it slow, doing maybe one crunch a week and then checking for unsightly bulges.

I belong to a gym and I often see personal trainers in action, tormenting their poorly dressed and pudgy customers. If you're the kind of person who hates other people, you should be a personal trainer. A personal trainer gets to hurt people physically *and* psychologically. The physical part is obvious: exercise hurts. The psychological part is that no matter how much the client exercises, he can never look like a personal trainer. So there's a sort of hopelessness built into the system. Lots of jobs allow you to hurt people physically—cops, dentists, and boxers come to mind—but only personal trainers get to make people feel bad emotionally too.

I've noticed that personal trainers like to make their victims do unconventional exercises that sometimes involve huge inflated balls, rope ladders, tennis balls, and poles, often in bizarre and frightening combinations. Usually the victims do these humiliating exercises right next to perfectly good exercise machines and weights. There are two possible explanations for why personal trainers eschew the machines and invent their own exercises for you:

1. Exercise equipment doesn't really work. No matter how many times you lift a heavy object, you will never get stronger. You will only become tired and injured.

Or . . .

2. Personal trainers are weasels. They know you won't pay them unless you think you're getting something special.

I would be the world's worst personal trainer. I would point to an exercise machine and say, "See the little picture of the guy on the side of the machine? Sit down and do what he's doing until you look like him." And if my client protested that I'm pointing to a picture of a skinless guy with no genitalia, I would say, "No pain no gain."

Smoking Weasels

Some industries have a higher weasel quotient than others. The food industry, for example, is 98 percent weasel, and I'm not just talking about the hot dogs. I have firsthand experience because in addition to my cartooning duties I own a food company that makes nutritious vegetarian burritos and a wheat-based protein ingredient for vegetarian cooking (see dilberito.com). I don't dare tell you any of my true experiences with food weasels because I'll be sued. So instead I'll use my constitutionally protected right to parody and tell you a totally false story of a completely fictitious company engaged in activities that never happened.

One day there was a large tobacco company that was doing an excellent job of killing the elderly, and they felt pretty good about that. But they weren't making enough progress injuring young people. So using their food company division, Krapped

Foods, they created a school lunch product made of lead chips, glue, and toenails. They flavored it with salt so it tasted delicious despite its limited nutritional content. They called the product Krapped Munchables, and it became a huge hit with busy mothers who were not fanatics about the health of their children. Soon there were new flavors of Krapped Munchables, including Fungus with Salt, Crud with Salt, and Rodent with Salt. Each was more delicious than the last.

But there was trouble on the horizon. A little upstart food company started producing highly nutritious vegetarian food, and this threatened to make the Krapped Munchables appear unhealthy by comparison. The little food company managed to sell its product to a huge convenience-store chain called 8-Twelve, where it appeared on the shelf right next to the Krapped Munchables. This was a major milestone for the little upstart food company, and they looked forward to making the world a better place by supplying nutritious and convenient food at a good price.

But after visiting a number of 8-Twelve stores, the little upstart company noticed a pattern. In each store they visited they found Krapped Munchables piled in front of their nutritious vegetarian product. Large companies that have hordes of brokers in the field sometimes use the weasel tactic of burying a competitor on the shelf. But the little upstart company knew that a big tobacco company would never do anything to hurt others. After a few months the 8-Twelve store realized it wasn't selling any nutritious vegetarian food and dropped the product to make room for the new line of Pus and Salt Krapped Munchables.

Dear Mr. Adams,

I worked at a concession stand in an ice arena. We sold soda for $1.50 while a vending machine about ten feet away sold the *exact* same drink for $1.00. So my weasel manager put up a sign on the vending machine saying Out of Order, though in fact nothing was wrong with the machine, forcing people to pay the extra fifty cents.

Political Weasels

If you accuse your neighbor of being a Satan worshiper, he'll sue you for slander. Unless he is one, in which case he'll use your entrails to decorate his mobile home and—depending how many entrails are left over—give his cat a snack. (Satan worshipers tend to be cat lovers.)

Either way it's better to keep your opinions about your neighbors to yourself. The exception to the rule is if your neighbor is a politician. Then you can say anything you want and it's not slander—it's simply "distorting the record," and it's completely legal.

Let's say you're running for office against a governor who eliminated poverty, paid for childhood vaccinations out of his own pocket, cut taxes, and balanced the budget. You can run ads on television that distort his record to something like "Governor supports legislation to execute innocent taxpayers!" While it's not technically "true," it's not slander because all you're doing is distorting the record. And since both sides do it, it's a level playing field and lawmakers find no reason to make it illegal.

The only problem with this system is that most voters are ignoramuses who get all of their opinions from paid TV ads. So the quality of political discourse tends to go like this:

Ignoramus 1: Which candidate do you like better—the shoplifter or the pedophile?

Ignoramus 2: Which one is the embezzler?

Ignoramus 1: According to the informative TV ads, both.

Ignoramus 2: I'll tell you one thing: I don't trust the ads from the Committee to Elect a Known Arsonist. They don't even have anything nice to say about their own candidate!

Ignoramus 1: Yeah, I picked up on that too.

Ignoramus 2: I'm tempted not to vote this year.

Ignoramus 1: *Get out of my house you Communist!*

The goal of every political campaign is to discourage voter turnout to the point where the candidate with the largest family wins. This is also known as the Kennedy Strategy.

Politicians have a weasel method of avoiding the truth without lying. It's called parsing, and you can do it too. The technique is to misinterpret questions as if you were an alien who had learned all of your language skills from reading a dictionary. Reporters are getting better at pinning down the politicians, so most interviews go like this:

Reporter: Senator, did you kill your wife?

Senator: I can't say for sure that I did.

> *Reporter:* Did you plunge a knife into her sixty-five times?
>
> *Senator:* I wasn't counting.
>
> *Reporter:* But a dozen witnesses saw you stab your wife with a knife until she died. Doesn't that mean you killed her?
>
> *Senator:* How do those witnesses know she wouldn't have died on her own? Are they doctors?
>
> *Reporter:* But you admit you stabbed your wife?
>
> *Senator:* No, the knife stabbed her. And I will not rest until that knife has been punished! I'm offering a $10,000 reward to anyone who can make the knife confess.

The worst way to run a country is to give voters useful information. For example, if a politician ever presented a complete list of national priorities, ranked in the order of how many people die from each, voters would kick him out of office. The list would look like this.

National Priorities

1. Stupidity

2. Eating too much food

3. Laziness

I don't think the government keeps statistics of how many people die from stupidity, but they should. It has to be a big number. I suppose the problem is that it's so subjective and you don't want to make the family members feel any worse.

Family Member: Oh my God! What happened, Officer?

           Cop: He died of stupidity.

Family Member: What?

           Cop: Yep. He drank a case of beer, hijacked a truck full of anvils, and tried to drive it across a frozen lake in April.

Family Member: Do you have to write it up that way? It sounds so cruel.

           Cop: No. I'll call it a driving accident.

It's illegal to kill yourself in a quick and painless way, but if you do it slowly over a few decades—say by not exercising—that's called laziness, not suicide, and it's completely legal. You might even get credit for being jolly or get a job as a TV chef on a cable network. When you die thirty years ahead of the average life expectancy, your obituary won't say, "Man dies of laziness." It will say, "Beloved TV chef succumbs to heart failure. He was removed from his bed with a crane."

My favorite thing that politicians say is "The voters aren't dumb." This is something that voters generally believe because they are dumb. I realize this sounds harsh. But if I'm wrong, and it's true that the voters are smart, despite all evidence to the contrary, it raises some troubling questions.

TROUBLING QUESTIONS

How uninformed must a voter be before it's okay to call him dumb?

If all the voters have roughly the same goals and the same information, but half of the voters vote one way and half vote the other way, doesn't that mean half of them are dumb?

How can we tell which half is the dumb half?

Healers

There's a religious guy on TV who scrunches up his face and prays for people to be healed. I worry that someday his prayers won't be aimed with the pinpoint accuracy that we all take for granted. What if he scrunches up his face wrong and it affects his aim. Could he make my neck double in size or make hair grow on the inside of my mouth? Perhaps you mock me for my concern, but if he can cure diseases by scrunching his face and muttering, he can certainly make a second nose grow out of my back.

I think the FDA should look into this healing-by-prayer technique and set some standards. TV healers should have warning labels on their foreheads, something along the lines of "Warning: TV healers might make your skull shrink to the size of a golf ball." I realize it's never happened, but I think you'll agree that just once would be too many.

And why is the healing limited to vital organs and major diseases? Suppose I wanted a haircut or a mole removed? Those things are important to me. It's not as if God is going to use up all his power on the little things and have nothing left over. He's omnipotent, and by definition that means he has plenty of power to spare. I see no reason that he can't shrink a tumor and clip my toenails at the same time.

News Makers

Sometimes when nothing interesting is happening anywhere on the planet, the media has to whip up some news to fill the void. The most popular method is to report on some new type of crime that most people have never even considered until they see it on TV. That gets the copycat criminals all riled up, and the next thing you know there's a national epidemic.

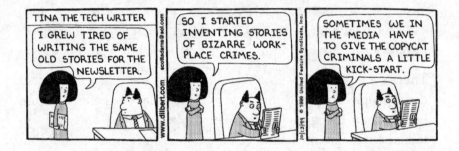

I don't blame the media for intentionally sparking crime sprees so they can sell ads. They have to do something because no one wants to hear a story about the link between quantum uncertainty and DNA mutations, for example. I wouldn't buy a car that was advertised on that kind of show. I want my commercials wrapped in stories like "Scientists try to clone cat but it comes out looking like Danny DeVito."

Experts

Television is full of experts lately. Experts generally say things that you and I could concoct while drinking enormous quantities of beer. Sometimes I like to watch the news and act as if it's a game show where I have to guess how the experts will answer the questions. It goes like this:

News Anchor:	Is it ever good to attack innocent people?
Me (at Home):	(guessing) Um . . . I think the expert will say no.
Expert:	We should do whatever we can to avoid it.
Me (at Home):	Woo-hoo! I'm still as smart as an expert! I believe I'll have another beer and try again.

Psychics

There's a guy on TV who can talk with the dead. It turns out that dead people are—and this is the hardest part to believe—more boring than living people. It seems that the dead only want to talk about nicknames, tattoos, old photographs, and health problems. And they are always happy. I want to see at least one episode where someone's dead grandma is screaming in agony as she slowly roasts in the flames of hell. I'm not mean-spirited; it's just that I think it would be good television. It seems highly coincidental to me that all dead people are happy about their situation. Personally, when my time comes, I'm not giving up that easily just because I'm dead. I plan to spend eternity trying to put my clothes back on.

Legal Weasels

If you want to avoid legal disputes in your business and financial life, you need to hire lawyers to negotiate contracts for you. The professional lawyer will turn your simple desires into a jumble of impenetrable weaseleze while siphoning off any excess money that he feels you didn't need. The better lawyers will make you feel weak and stupid and helpless.

> **Lawyer:** Does this clause look good to you?
> **You:** Um . . . I don't understand a single word it says. It seems to be written in Klingon. It's almost as if you're intentionally trying to confuse me.
> **Lawyer:** Maybe I should work on it for a few more hours at $350 per hour until you understand it.
> **You:** *It's good! It's good! I understand it now!*

When the contract is done, neither you nor the other side will ever want to deal with lawyers again as long as you live. That's why contracts are effective for avoiding future disputes.

A defense attorney (weasel extraordinaire) will publicly support a client's story if it doesn't sound too laughably unbelievable. But every once in a while you hear about some miscreant who, for example, commits multiple murders at the National Video Camera Convention and leaves ten fingerprints, three cups of DNA, five thousand eyewitnesses, sixty-five video recordings, and a taped confession at the crime scene. The defense lawyer knows he'll look like a complete idiot if he says, "My client is innocent." Instead he'll weasel-word it:

"My client *says* he didn't do it."

"There is a rush to judgment."

"The police refuse to follow up leads on other suspects."

A wonderful defense-lawyer trick is to give a lie detector test to a guilty client and then tell the media he passed. As you probably know, courts don't allow evidence from lie detector tests. I'm no expert in lie detectors, but I can think of two possible explanations why the court system doesn't value this input:

1. Judges prefer the challenge of making decisions without information.

Or . . .

2. Scientists have performed controlled experiments on lie detector tests and found that they *don't work.*

You might think that when the media covers this sort of story, they would seek out the scientists who have tested the reliability of lie detectors and then pass that important contextual information to their viewers. But hunting down those scientists would be a lot of work. So instead, the media look in the Yellow Pages under "lie detector" and trot out a bunch of people who *make their living giving lie detector tests.* Then the media ask the people who *make their living giving lie detector tests* if the method is reliable. They usually say yes.

Real Estate Weasels

Here's some career advice for you. An ideal job would be the kind where you only deal with frightened and uninformed customers who are willing to spend huge amounts of money. I can think of two jobs that fit that description. If you would enjoy wearing drab clothing and ripping out people's guts only to replace them with other people's guts or parts from animals or experimental gadgets, then you can be a transplant surgeon. But if you're squeamish and you would rather wear nice clothes and drive around in a Mercedes-Benz, and you didn't do that well in school, I recommend becoming a real estate broker.

Some people think that a Realtor's top priority is to find the best home for a prospective buyer. That would require looking at every available home until the client dies of old age, because if the client actually bought something, it would ruin the possibility of finding a better choice next week. So clearly it's impractical for the Realtor to help find the "best" home. A more practical approach is to whip the client into a frenzy of desire and stress until his brain stem takes control of the decision-making.

The seasoned Realtor knows from the subtle cues given by the client when a buying decision is near. For example, a client who is *not* yet ready to buy might use the analytical part of the brain and say something like "I wonder if this property has all of the required building permits filed with the city." But a client who is ready to buy will grunt like a hog and roll around on the carpet.

The home-buying market would collapse if Realtors tried to give clients what they want. Because what they want is the Hearst Castle for $20,000, a ten-year warranty on major appliances, and a sensual back rub from the title company. Instead, Realtors take the more reasoned approach of making the buyers want whatever is available. This involves first showing the client some "affordable" homes that are constructed entirely from crushed beer cans and rolled newspapers. By the fourth house visit the client is willing to become a thief to afford a home that has central heating and a roof.

Here's an example of a Realtor who did not properly condition her client.

Dear Mr. Adams,

My wife and I are thinking about selling our home and buying another, but we weren't in any hurry. We enlisted a Realtor to help.

She gave us her opinion of the value of our property. It was $100,000 less than the house around the corner that sold a month earlier. She encouraged us to list our home for *less than that* to encourage a quick sale. She also encouraged us to offer more than the asking price for a new house we liked in order to assure that we would get it.

In other words, she advised us to sell our home for less than it's worth and buy the other for more than it is worth, in order for her to get a quick commission on both transactions.

At the end of the house-buying process the buyer is escorted to a small conference room and shown a three-foot-tall stack of incomprehensible documents to sign. Just for fun, next time you buy a house, look at the documents and say to your Realtor, "I'd like to read these carefully before signing." Then take the top document and read it out loud as if you had been taught to read by Coco the gorilla. Sound out the bigger words and ask probing questions like "What is meant by *the?* I see that word a lot."

Home Improvements and Service People

If you hire someone to install a new carpet in your house, he will damage your wallboards. If you make him repair the wallboards, he will damage your wall. If you give up on the original guy and hire a wall-fixer, he will paint your electrical outlets shut and destroy your new carpet, and so on into infinity, until eventually you have destroyed your entire home and are forced to live in a cave and eat bugs.

Home repair: The process of destroying portions of your home that were minding their own business.

Service people are weasels. They know that if they were to spend the time and money to repair all the things they have accidentally destroyed, the entire economy of the world would grind to a halt. All forms of commerce would end as angry consumers demanded satisfaction. Luckily for the world, lots of people, like me, would rather look at a gash in the wall for the rest of their life than have this conversation:

Me:	You put a hole in my wall. I demand that you fix it.
Carpet Guy:	No, I didn't. That hole was already there.
Me:	I saw you do it. I was standing right here.
Carpet Guy:	I don't know what you're talking about.
Me:	Yes, you do. Your arm is still stuck in the hole up to your shoulder and you were just yelling, "@ %&$, I put a hole in the wall!"

Carpet Guy:	Okay, for the sake of argument, let's say I did put a slight hole in the wall. You can't really see it.
Me:	That's because your arm is in it! I demand that you remove your arm from my wall and fix that hole!
Carpet Guy:	If I fix the hole, I will lose money on this job! I have a family to feed!
Me:	Oh . . . Okay. I didn't know about the family.
Carpet Guy:	Apology accepted.

Service people for your home also have their own notion of time. When they say, "I'll be here at 9 A.M. on Monday," that translates to "I'll be here sometime before the sun shrinks to the size of a Tic Tac, unless I have family problems or truck problems or another job runs late or the distributor doesn't have the part I need or it rains."

And the phrase "I'll call you if my plans change" translates roughly to "I don't have a to-do list. I just do whatever makes people stop yelling at me. You might try to call me and yell at me, but no one will answer the phone."

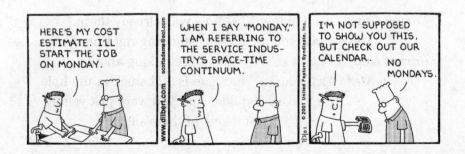

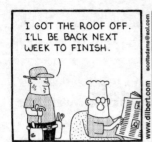
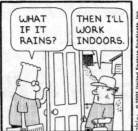
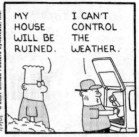

23

Philosophy of Weasels

In this chapter I will discuss some of the larger philosophical issues in the field of weasel studies.

The Viking System

Weasels can only thrive in civilized societies where there are laws against slaying people simply because you think they deserve it. That's why, for example, you never hear stories involving elderly Viking weasels. Weasels didn't last that long under the Viking system. Business transactions went like this:

> ***Weasel:*** Hey, Thor, may I polish your sword?
> ***Thor:*** How much will that cost?
> ***Weasel:*** It's totally free.
> ***Thor:*** Wow! Okay.

(Next day)

> ***Thor:*** I'm here to pick up my polished sword.
> ***Weasel:*** Sure. That'll cost you three goats for overnight storage.
> ***Thor:*** What? You said it was free!
> ***Weasel:*** I said the *polishing* was free.

At that point Thor would run his sword through the weasel, lift him in the air, let out an impressive Norse yelp, and fling the limp carcass on a thatched roof a block away. This is one example in which the Viking system was better.

Capitalism

The Viking system eventually gave way to something called capitalism. Economists have explained the wonders of capitalism in books so thick and dreadful that their own editors gouge their eyes out halfway through the first chapter. But that's okay because, generally speaking, anything that takes a whole book to explain is wrong anyway. Luckily for you I have a shorter definition of capitalism that is right on the money.

Capitalism: A system in which weasels sell crap to each other.

Let's face it—if people didn't buy crap, the entire economy would collapse, because crap is the only thing for sale. For example, I'm typing this book on a computer that crashes six times a day. The computer sits on my desk next to my defective telephone (replaced twice this year), which is sitting next to my defective TV remote control (replaced three times this year), which only occasionally operates my erratic television system (six repairs this year). I didn't make up any of that, by the way.*

If I weren't willing to buy defective products, I'd be sitting in

---

*I used the favorite research method of the professional writer, i.e., looking at whatever is sitting on my desk.

an empty room starving to death. Wait . . . no, I take that back; the room wouldn't be here either. Allow me to explain.

When I was finalizing the deal to buy my house, I was sitting in the kitchen with my real estate agent and a house inspector when a rainstorm broke out—*in the kitchen.* The ceiling started spewing gallons of water from each of the recessed light fixtures. I don't mean to sound picky. After all, it was raining outside too—fair enough—but still, you don't expect rain to reach the ground floor of a two-story home without at least getting slowed down by a mattress or a carpet on the upper floor. It was a frightening thing to behold, but not as frightening as the look on the face of the real estate broker, who tried to maintain an expression on her face that said, "All great houses do this sort of thing. Give me my commission, you anal-retentive bastard."

Was I deterred from buying the house just because the kitchen ceiling had better water pressure than the showers? Heck no. I figured all the other houses in the world have their own problems, and at least with this house I knew where to put the buckets.

Free Speech

If you're reading this book, you probably live in a country that has freedom of speech. But there are still some things you'd better not say. For example, you can't yell "Fire!" in a crowded theater. You can't say "Mayday" on the radio just for fun. You can't joke about anthrax in the lunchroom. You can't describe your genitalia to your coworkers. You can't threaten to hurt someone. You can't say you're a cop if you're not. You can't lie under oath. You can't curse too much on television. You can't insult minorities. You can't slander. You can't complain about your employer without getting fired. You can't insult gang members and live. You can't mention bombs at the airport. And you can't solicit sex for money.

That eliminates most of the things you want to say. But there are still a few things that are totally protected speech:

1. Asking people to hand you things

2. Talking to yourself when no one is listening

3. Complaining about the government

4. Singing along with the radio

5. Yelling at pets

6. Convincing people to buy crap

The first five items don't occupy much of your day unless you have very short arms and can't reach things or you own a cat. But the last item on the list is the primary topic of all human communication. That's why my definition of free speech is this.

Free speech: The things you say to get people to buy crap.

Here I am not limiting my discussion to the purchases of shoddy merchandise. I'm referring to any situation where you want someone to think something is better than it really is. That includes your clownlike physical appearance, your annoying personality, your ridiculous opinions, and your job performance. After all, the most defective products that we sell are ourselves.

Even when you're complaining about how *bad* something is, you're really just using a weasel method to explain how *wonderful* you are in comparison. Think about it—if you say your boss is an idiot, you're saying you could do his job better. If you say your car is terrible, you're saying you deserve a nicer one. In a sense, all complaints are just ways of complimenting yourself. If you were less weaselly, you might say, "My car is worthless and defective, but that's okay because so am I." You never hear that.

The hardest selling you'll ever do is your very first job interview. That's when you have no work experience, so your product (yourself) is at its height of defective glory. You have to compensate with extra weaseling. Let me tell you my story as an example of successful weaseling.

A week after I graduated from college I traded my rusty car to my little sister for a one-way plane ticket to California. (Sucker!) I took with me all of my worldly possessions: I had the finest three-piece suit that money could buy, assuming you only used your money to buy merchandise made of recycled plastic bags. I had one suitcase lovingly crafted from the leather of diseased* zoo animals. And I had $2,000 to last me the rest of my life. I was hoping it was enough to retire because the idea of working didn't appeal to me.

I spent the first week in Los Angeles sleeping on my older brother's couch in a sleeping bag filled with cracker crumbs. I assume that whenever my brother got the urge to eat crackers, he unrolled his sleeping bag and used it as a bib. Or maybe

*Whatever disease turns animals yellow.

(because my brother is an inspiration to all weasels) he put the crumbs in there before I arrived to hasten my departure. All I know is that once the crumbs were in there, it was easier to sleep on them than to pick them out with tweezers.

Retirement wasn't working out the way I'd planned, so I decided to throw away the rest of my life by getting a job. I set up interviews with two banks. The first bank offered me a job sitting in a windowless basement for twelve hours a day analyzing large mounds of documents for no apparent reason. I don't remember the details of the interview, but I probably expressed my lifetime desire to analyze huge mounds of documents in a windowless basement, and that impressed the interviewer so much that he offered me the job. I enthusiastically accepted and agreed to report to work on Monday.

Then I went to my next job interview. I forget the details of that job opportunity—it might have involved driving nails into my own skull—but they said they would give me more money than the windowless-basement job so I accepted and agreed to report to work on Monday.

In my remaining days of prework freedom I flew to San Francisco to see an ex-girlfriend who had begged me to visit. She said she would meet me at the airport, but sometime during my flight she changed her mind and decided to stay home and watch television instead. So there I was at the San Francisco airport, wearing my one plastic suit, carrying a diseased-leather bag containing all of my possessions except one—I had forgotten my address book. And my ex-girlfriend—the only person I knew in San Francisco—wasn't listed in the phone book. After a few hours of waiting at the airport I decided to take a chance and hunt her down at what I fuzzily recalled might be her address. I wasn't what you would call "street-smart," so my travels from the airport via public transportation took me to the Sixteenth and Mission BART station. A cheerful group of homeless people surrounded me to look at my plastic suit and try to dislodge me from my diseased-leather suitcase. I wasn't buying the story that they were bellhops. I held on to my suitcase while they dragged me out of the station and onto the sidewalk. Luckily a policeman wandered by and shooed them away, probably so he could get a better look at my plastic suit and yellow luggage.

Somehow I found my ex-girlfriend's apartment and she was home. I asked her why she hadn't met me at the airport or at least left a message. She explained—and I believed her—that she didn't feel like it. She said I could stay with her if I liked. She had a sleeping bag full of crumbs that I could sleep in. My first impressions of San Francisco were so enjoyable (nice people!) that the next day I woke up, brushed off the crumbs, and went downtown to apply for a job.

I got in line at a branch office of Crocker Bank, and then, using the old bait-and-switch routine, I asked for a job instead of making a huge deposit. I was ushered into the back room and interviewed minutes later. For some reason they were having trouble finding college-educated people who would work for $650 per month. They offered me a job as a bank teller and I accepted. I agreed to report to work on Monday.

So far I had three jobs that all started on Monday. I hadn't worked a single day in my adult life and already I was screwing two employers—three if you count the suckers who actually ended up with me on the payroll. Strictly speaking, I wasn't lying when I told each of them I would report to work on Monday. Each time I said it, I meant it. It was weaselly to look for a job after accepting a job, but totally acceptable behavior under the wonderful system of capitalism. I figured that if the capitalists who offered me those jobs didn't like capitalism, they wouldn't have named the system after themselves.

Speaking of fairness . . .

Fairness: A sensation you get when you have all the stuff you started with plus at least 50 percent of someone else's stuff.

For example, let's say a man and a woman are having a discussion about the fact that women are paid less for doing the same jobs as men. The "fairness" argument goes like this:

> ***Woman:*** Women should be paid the same as men for doing the same work! It's only fair!
>
> ***Man:*** Sounds good to me. While we're talking about fairness, women should pay just as much as men for car insurance, and they should kill half of the spiders in the house.
>
> ***Woman:*** Stop changing the subject!

That example sounds sexist. In the interest of fairness I will make the same point by flipping it around. Let's say a man is complaining that men always have to lift all the heavy objects while women stand around pointing and objecting to the way the object is being moved.

> ***Man:*** Women should lift heavy objects themselves instead of asking men to do it! It's only fair.

> **Woman:**　Sounds good to me. While we're at it, maybe you could give birth to the next generation of human beings.
>
> **Man:**　Stop changing the subject!

In reality, the only person who wants *real* fairness is whoever has the worst life on earth, because he has nothing of his own to share in return. I don't know who that person is, but I have a mental image of a naked guy with no arms and legs, living in a rented poison ivy patch and being forced to read this book. Now, *that* guy wants *real* fairness.

24

The Weasel Mind

The fastest way to spot a weasel is to look at a shiny surface. The second-fastest way is to look for people who are certain about the future. When a person conveys a sense of certainty during times of great uncertainty, that is either a sign of mental illness called "leadership" or a sign of a weasel who is trying to get his way.

For example, take the issue of drilling for oil in the Arctic National Wildlife Refuge. The weasels on both sides of the issue exhibit freakish levels of certainty about the future, but in opposite directions. The weasels that favor drilling say, in effect, "It won't have any impact on the critters that live there. To caribou, oil tastes like chocolate milk."

The opponents of drilling say, in effect, "Any critters that escape the uncontrolled oil-well fires that will surely blot out the sun will be hunted down individually, their hands and feet tied with pipe cleaners, and WD-40 injected directly into their bloodstreams." I'm paraphrasing, but trust me, there's a lot of certainty on both sides.

I can see why weasels would avoid talking about probability. As soon as you bring probability into your argument, you sound unpersuasive no matter which side you're on. See for yourself:

Side 1:
"There's only a 10 percent chance that our drilling will
decimate wildlife in that area for a million years. Okay,
okay, more like 60 percent if no one is looking. But we like
those odds because we don't live there."

Or . . .

Side 2:
"There's a 10 percent chance we can convince the weasel
public to stop guzzling oil and use conservation to forestall
a global meltdown. And 10 percent is good, isn't it?"

See? Both arguments seem unpersuasive when you bring
probability into the picture.

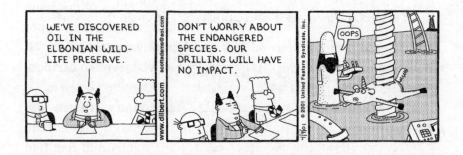

I realize that some readers will hallucinate that my political
opinion on oil drilling is embedded in what I've just written and
they will feel disturbed that I am misleading the public. If this
describes you, feel free to write and tell me that Dilbert books
are not 100 percent accurate. I like getting funny e-mail.

Weasel Wisdom

If you take complete nonsense and turn it into a popular saying, that's called weasel wisdom. Here is a small sample of weasel wisdom.

The simplest explanation is usually correct.

In my experience, the simplest explanation is the one that comes out of the mouth of the most clueless person. If you ask a physicist why a rock falls to the ground, he's going to spend three days with charts and equations and stories about Newton and Einstein and string theory until you want to beat him senseless with the rock. If you ask a clueless guy, he'll say, "Because the rock is heavy." That's why I'm skittish about accepting the simplest explanation. Or the most complicated one. Something in the middle range usually works for me.

If it walks like a duck and quacks like a duck, it's a duck.

Yes, most things that waddle and quack are indeed ducks. But sometimes it's a duck hunter who just got a vicious wedgie from the other hunters while simultaneously blowing into a duck call. If you think that isn't happening daily, then obviously you haven't been duck hunting with me.

It's a slippery slope.

Everything can sound like a slippery slope if you want it to. For example, I was scared when NASA gathered rocks from the moon because what's to stop them from stealing the entire thing, one bucket at a time? I'd hate to look up there one night and see a blank space where the moon used to be. And I never wear a sweatband when I play tennis because I'm afraid that's how King Tut got on the slippery slope to becoming a mummy.

If you give a man a fish, he will eat for a day. Teach him to fish and he will eat forever.

You can test the wisdom of the "teach a man to fish" saying the next time you find a starving man. Offer to set up a time when you can get together so you can teach him to fish. I think a two-day seminar on the basics should be enough, covering the ins and outs of tackle and bait and, of course, fishing etiquette.

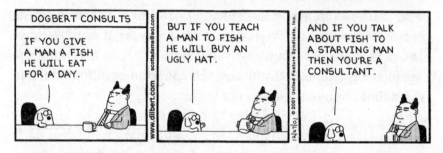

If all you have is a hammer, everything looks like a nail.

Maybe it's because I'm shy, but if all I had were a hammer (no clothes), I'd be using that hammer to cover my naughty bits while I ran behind a tree. I doubt I'd be thinking, "No one can see me. It's just a bunch of nails out there."

It is better to ask forgiveness than to seek approval.

Sometimes, in special cases, it's better to ask forgiveness than to seek approval. That special case would be if you expect your boss to leave the company before you get caught. For all other times it's better to ask permission, get turned down, and then blame a coworker when things go wrong.

Humans only use 10 percent of their brains.

Hardly a day passes without our hearing, "We only use ten percent of our brains." The implication is that if we tapped into the other 90 percent of our noggins, we could levitate objects, understand Dennis Miller, calculate a 15 percent tip, and divide it by four coworkers. The latter talent would be quite useless once you could levitate objects; you'd never have to pay for food again. If you got hungry, you could just levitate a zebra from the zoo directly onto your barbecue grill. But the point is, it's commonly understood that 90 percent of your brain isn't pulling its weight. And like all common understandings, it's a myth, according to the *Skeptical Inquirer.** Apparently the origin of the 10 percent estimate was "some guy who thought it sounded good."

In reality your brain is busy all the time doing the sort of thing that mine did a minute ago. (True story coming up.) I was all tuckered out from working late last night so I climbed onto my freakishly oversize hassock for a quick nap. As I often do, I entered a topic into my mind so that my subconscious could come up with creative solutions and ideas while I slept. When I woke up, amazingly, this thought was in my head:

Question: Where's Prince Albert?

Answer: He's in the can.

That's it. All I had was a slight variation of a famous telephone prank call. I think this proves that 100 percent of my

---

*The *Skeptical Inquirer* is a magazine for skeptics. I have an uneasy feeling that everything in it is completely made up, but I don't know what magazine to read to find out.

brain was already busy and had no extra space for solving problems. I don't know what else my brain needed to do while I napped, but I suspect that at least 75 percent of the job was trying to limit the drool damage to my hassock.

Some people are more afraid of public speaking than dying.

One way to check that theory would be to offer to kill people who are scheduled to do speeches. You'd have to make the offer to a hundred people to get a decent sample. If seventy of them say, "Thank you. Please do it now," then I think there's some merit to this wisdom. Otherwise it's weasel wisdom. I realize the original "fear of speaking" theory was based on some sort of survey. I'd love to see the meeting where the researcher who did that study first showed the results to the department.

Researcher: Surprisingly, the data show that people fear public speaking more than they fear death.

Coworker: When you say "people," are you referring exclusively to morons?

Researcher: No, no. I mean ordinary people like you and me.

Coworker: Okay, would you rather finish your presentation or have us storm the podium and kill you?

Researcher: Um . . . dang, now I'm locked into my own argument. I guess I want you to kill me. I hope I don't regret this later.

(Sounds of struggle)

Coworker: (breathing hard) Wow! That was the most persuasive presentation I've ever seen!

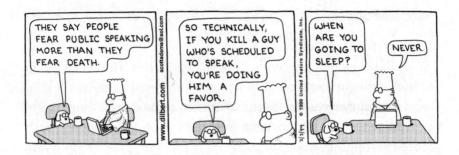

There is one special person for everyone.

They say there's one soul mate for every person. The part I don't understand is why your soul mate usually lives or works within driving distance. I mean, why isn't your soul mate sometimes a Hmong mountain person in Laos? Or even worse than geographic undesirability would be this:

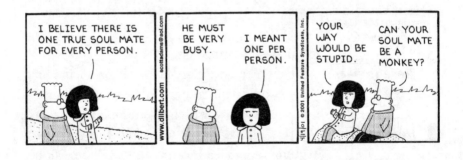

And why is it that when married people get divorced, they generally find a new soul mate—the emergency spare soul mate—who *also lives nearby?* The soul mate system must be very efficient.

Weasel Rage

Weasels try to be enraged as often as possible because it feels good. But they quickly run out of reasons in the "righteous indignation" category and need to branch out. Road rage was a godsend for angry weasels. It sounds almost clinical, as if there might be a pill to treat it, and therefore no one's fault. Road rage is much more reasonable sounding than "angry jerk in a car." People will admit to road rage, but not to being an angry jerk in a car.

I think this concept should be expanded to other fields. For example, I get mad when I can't open a jar without resorting to some sort of girly-girl prosthetic jar-opening device. I huff and puff and I turn red and want to throw the jar against a wall. But I don't because I would be considered an "angry jerk who couldn't open a jar." That sounds bad. I prefer to be accused of jar rage. That's got a nice ring. I might even get pills.

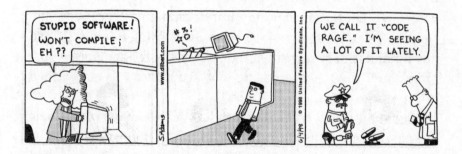

Basket Case Theory

Back when I was young and dating, i.e.; a serial loser, I developed what I called the basket case theory. This elegant theory states that all women seem normal at first but are basket cases when you get to know them. The same is true of men, but thanks to the miracle of low expectations, no one seems to care. Obviously I was a basket case too, as proven by the fact that I was bitter enough to create this theory. Thank goodness I'm completely normal now.

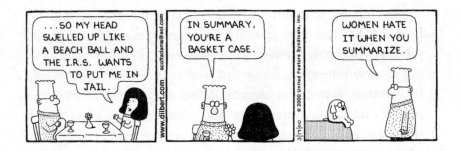

It's easy to like people you've just met. They're all smiley and friendly and their nutty secrets are cleverly concealed. But after you get to know someone, the inner lunatic emerges. You discover that the person you respected for sticking to a disciplined low-fat diet is in reality suffering from obsessive-compulsive disorder and can't eat anything but fruit that's been washed twenty-three times.

Sigmund Freud had some insightful ideas about why people are basket cases. But he didn't write any of it down because he was busy snorting cocaine and dating his mother. By contrast I have a lot of free time so I'll offer my insight instead: When humans are in the womb, they are little more than blobs of mindless and irrational gooky stuff. Eventually they get larger. That's all you need to know.

Jobs can be basket cases too. You can divide all jobs into two categories:

1. **Good jobs**
2. **Bad jobs**

Good jobs are defined as the ones that other people have. Bad jobs are the ones *you* have. That's not a coincidence. Every job looks like easy money until you've been at it a few days. During the job interview, when you look at the cubicle where you'll be working, your brain imagines what it would be like to sit happily in that comfy chair, stimulated by the intellectual challenge of the job and amused by the banter of your carefree coworkers. Your brain doesn't have the capacity to imagine yourself being emotionally abused every day for thirty years, and every night fantasizing about passing away in your sleep.

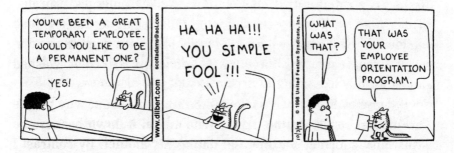

Self-Weaseling

I sometimes wonder who among the billions of workers in the world has the very worst job on earth. And what exactly is that job? I have great sympathy whoever it is because the job probably involves a combination of animal guts, low pay, and breathing toxic fumes in a windowless, radioactive room, with a boss who continuously loses money betting on tape-delayed sporting events. Whatever it is, I'll bet the person doing the job is thinking it's not so bad. That's how people are. We self-weasel, i.e., delude ourselves into thinking that whatever we're doing is okay.

Thank goodness for self-weaseling. Otherwise no one would do all the jobs for which I—and people like me—are unqualified. Those jobs include anything where you're not supposed to be lazy, frightened of all forms of danger including some that are just imagined, easily grossed out, unwilling to use substandard bathroom facilities, unable to lift heavy objects, easily sunburned, and allergic to almost everything.

There are millions of unpleasant jobs, and yet I can't think of a single one that is going undone because no one is willing to do it. Take the job of prison guard. Who wakes up one day and thinks, "A good job might be one that involves being in a prison all day long with angry psychopaths who have friends on the outside who will learn where my family lives." To most of us so-called normal people, it seems that being a prison guard is almost exactly like being in prison except you also have the hassle of a commute.

I'm not complaining, just amazed that people *choose* unpleasant careers. Consider the person who stands at highway construction sites and holds the Slow sign for motorists. Every person in that job at one time probably thought, "Hey, that looks easy. I can hold a little sign." And indeed it is easy for the first ten to twelve minutes. After that you really want to sit down. Standing in one place for a long time is hard. If you don't believe me, try this exercise at home: stand in one place for eight hours holding a sign that says Slow. By the seventh hour you'll be thinking, "That cartoonist is always right. I wish I could be more like him."

And of course you need to consider the ridicule factor when you enter the sign-holding profession. If you are unfortunate enough to have a face that looks even the slightest bit—how can I say—"dopey," it's a bad idea to stand in public with a sign that says Slow. As a typical motorist with an evil sense of humor, I can vouch that this intersection of dopey* face and ironic signage has not been lost on me.

Commuters are another group that do a heroic job of self-weaseling. Somehow they have to convince themselves that spending four hours a day in cars, buses, streetcars, trains, and subways is better than the alternative of being, for example, a professional taster at a glue factory that's within walking distance of your house.

Commuting is the ultimate revenge of the inner-city folks. They're saying, in their own inimitable way, "You can have a great job and a great house, but if you put them near each other, we'll kill you." As a general rule, most criminals are located between your workplace and your house. That's why you need to transport yourself inside a metal container of some sort, i.e., a car, SUV, train, subway, or armored bodysuit.

The easiest and most rewarding target for your weasel methods is your future self. For example, you could convince yourself

*I'm not saying all sign-holders are dopey. I'm saying they're all dopey *looking*.

that changing the oil in your car is optional. The *current you* will save money and time. The only victim will be the *future you,* and frankly, that weasel would do the same thing to you if time flowed in the opposite direction.

So go ahead and convince yourself to overeat, smoke, drink too much, and have sex without protection. And always remember the mantra of successful self-weasels: "The long run is for losers."

Weasel Drug Makers

I have a continuous itch in the middle of my back. This wouldn't be a problem for anyone with flexible muscles. But I can barely scratch my forehead without snapping a tendon. Reaching the middle of my back is out of the question. I squirm and rub against inanimate objects all day, searching, always searching, for the perfect hard corner about shoulder-high. And let me tell you, there is a theoretical amount of itchiness that will erase any fear of embarrassment: you will interrupt a wedding to walk up to the altar and rub against the decorative trellis like a cow on a fence post. You might even moo.

So I bought an anti-itch cream. The instructions say to apply it five times a day. This was a red flag for me because I think like a weasel and I suspect everyone else of being a weasel. If I were going to sell an anti-itch cream that didn't work, I'm sure I would recommend applying it five times a day. I figure no consumer has that sort of energy, so he'll blame himself when it doesn't work.

That leaves me with plan B, which involves growing my fingernails five inches long and hoping they curl in the right direction.

And now, excuse me while I use my keyboard to scratch my back. Ahhh . . . yqaoeiu87alk3'asllkj96q8572;s,mrk . . . *moo!*

Parental Weasels

I used to be puzzled that, whenever I saw a baby in a restaurant, it would be banging the table with a spoon, nonstop, for about an hour. It's always a spoon, rarely a fork or a knife, so I know there's some conscious decision making involved. Restaurant managers never try to stop the banging, probably because grabbing a baby and shaking it is considered bad customer service. So the other patrons are treated to a musical show that is as relaxing as the sound of a guy beating on the inside of his coffin, but without the vocal accompaniment of *"I'm alive!!! I'm alive!!!"*

I assumed all babies bang spoons instinctively. Recently I discovered the weasel-truth. Mothers have figured out that if the baby is banging a spoon on the table, he isn't doing something worse, and babies have *lots* of worse tricks. Mothers are somewhat immune to the noise produced by their own offspring. By giving the baby a spoon, the mother can happily enjoy her meal while the baby bangs away.

One of my favorite local restaurants sounds like a continuous performance of *Riverdance.* Mothers hand spoons to their babies as soon as they sit down. (This is literally true.) When the glaring from other customers gets too intense, the mothers will sometimes quietly scold the babies. But babies are weasels too, and they understand that they won't be punished for acting like babies. So pretty soon they start squealing, the weasel parents give in and hand the baby a spoon, and the cycle of angry stares continues.

My question is this: Shouldn't all restaurants come equipped with padded spoons for babies? They could bang all day and it wouldn't make much noise. If the baby really needs to hear the noise, then I recommend little baby headphones with fake noise piped in. C'mon, they're babies—they won't know the difference!

25

The Sign of the Weasel

Have you ever made the "You're a loser" hand signal? That's the one where you make an *L* with your thumb and forefinger and hold it up to your forehead. This is one of the great inventions of the last hundred years. It's completely free and it's a guaranteed laugh. It only has one drawback: if you accidentally use the wrong hand to make the signal it forms a backward *L* and it comes off as sadly ironic. Still, there's a 50 percent chance you'll get it right, and those are good odds for something that's free.

Along similar lines, wouldn't it be great if there were some sort of universal hand signal that says, "You're a weasel"? This signal would have many uses. For example, imagine you're in a business meeting and one of your diabolical coworkers suggests a brilliant weasel solution to an otherwise intractable problem. Everyone sits in stunned silence, marveling at the majesty and beauty of the weasel's plan. Then someone in the meeting—let's say you—punctuates the moment by making the universal Sign of the Weasel. Hilarity ensues. Suddenly your coworkers realize that you are witty and extraordinarily sexy. Within days everyone in the office has plastic surgery to look more like you. Wouldn't that be great?

Here's my suggestion for the Sign of the Weasel. I have been trying this out at home with much success. It's all predicated on the belief that weasels have whiskers like a cat. This may or may not be the case. You might think that an author who writes an entire book about weasels would know one way or the other. But let's not dwell on that. The important thing is that other people don't know if weasels have whiskers. The Sign of the Weasel goes like this:

1. Take your left hand and form the peace sign (two fingers out) down by your side. Those fingers will become your simulated weasel whiskers. Sweep your hand up to your nose so the fingers point out to your right. This will form one-half of the simulated weasel whiskers. Make a sound effect like Zorro's sword moving through the air, roughly like *fft*.

2. Quickly do the same thing with your right hand, including the sound effect, until it crosses with the left hand under the nose. Your weasel whiskers are now complete. The left hand forms the whiskers on the right of your face and the right hand forms the left whiskers.

I have experimented doing the hand signal without the sound effect, and it isn't nearly as good. The *fft-fft* really brings it home. When you are done, it should look like this:

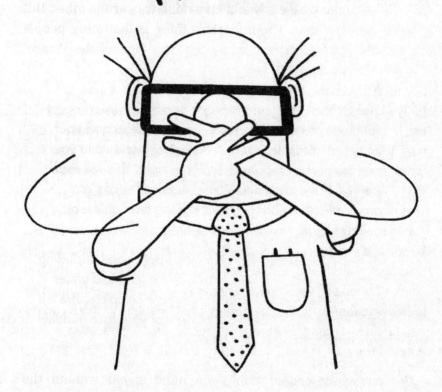

26

Weasel Abuse

If you're normal, sometimes you wake up with an urge to verbally abuse people. But you probably don't, because most people are in a position to get revenge if you make the first move. That's why it's a good thing that vendors and salespeople exist. Customers are expected to abuse vendors and salespeople. And that's okay because the price of the abuse is built right into the cost of the product.

For example, a car would normally only cost about $25 because it's made entirely from stuff found in the ground—ore, sand, petroleum, etc. All the rest of the markup is labor and a surcharge for taking verbal abuse. All day long the salespeople have to hear customers whining—things like "I paid forty thousand dollars for this piece of $#*!! and all four wheels fell off when I drove it out of the parking lot!" I feel sorry for salespeople, like this one:

Dear Mr. Adams,

We received this today at my company:
    "Effective immediately!
    "Please refrain from making abusive and derogatory statements to the copier repairman. He has come to me to

complain about the great number of people making rude comments to him about the copier and has stressed that they want the copier to work just as much as we do. Specifically, please do not suggest that he toss the copier down the elevator shaft. This comment hurt his feelings.

"Thanks for your cooperation."

Weasel Directions

Recently I was planning for a meeting in San Francisco and I called to ask for driving directions. I forgot a basic rule of weaseldom, that the person you ask for directions has one of two possible motives:

1. Help you reach your destination

Or . . .

2. Send you to discover the actual physical path to hell

If you're smart, you ask directions from the person who invited you to the meeting. That person *wants* you to reach your destination. If you're dumb, as I was, you ask whoever answers the phone. In my case it was the receptionist. As a general rule, the receptionist doesn't care if you live or die. And she certainly doesn't care *where* you live or die. She just wants you to get off the phone.

The receptionist of my story used a classic weasel maneuver and sent me to the Internet for my driving directions, to a popular Web site that has on-line maps and driving directions.

Now, I've tried getting driving instructions from Internet map sites many times. Maybe there's something strange about where I live, but I find that my directions always include at least one "Turn left at Unknown." I usually notice that problem when I'm halfway to my destination.

Secondly, if you're viewing a crowded metropolitan area, the map automatically leaves off some detail to make it more readable. For example, the map leaves off the street names. You can print out all the various levels of details to get all the street names if you have the time. But that takes roughly the same amount of time as:

1. Cloning famous explorers Lewis and Clark

2. Sending them on an expedition to locate your destination

3. Waiting for the carrier pigeon to return with their instructions

That's why I use the antiweasel triangulation method whenever I'm getting directions. First I ask for directions from the person that invited me. Then I call the hotel or restaurant and ask directions. Then I use my map software. All three sources will give me different directions, with at least two of the three being wrong. The well-meaning person that invited me might have forgotten a street. The map software sends me to "unknown" places, and the hotel person is a weasel. But if I piece together all the directions, then look at a map, I'll only have to stop two or three times along the way.

Sometimes on the way you have to phone your intended destination and make them confess that their original directions were bad.

Me:	I'm at Oak Street like you said, but it dead-ends and there is no Willow Avenue.
Weasel:	Yes, there is. I use it every day. You are either blind or stupid.
Me:	No, there isn't. I carefully cataloged each cross street along the entire length of Oak and put them in alphabetical order. There is no Willow Avenue.
Weasel:	Oh, that's right! Ha ha! I meant Walnut Avenue!

Men are often criticized for being reluctant to stop and ask for directions. The popular belief is that we're stubborn. That's only part of the reason. When I get lost, everyone on the street starts to look like a psycho, lying weasel. And by that I mean more than usual.

Training Your Boss to Accept Abuse

It's both fun and satisfying to verbally abuse your boss. But it's a bad career strategy unless you train him/her first. The trick is to start with tiny witticisms about a harmless aspect of your boss's personality and then expand from there. For example, if your boss likes fishing, you could insert harmless fish-related "jokes" into the meeting.

Boss:	I think we have a big opportunity with this customer.
You:	You mean big like that fish you allegedly caught? Ha ha!

It's not funny but neither will it end your career. It's just a test. If your boss smiles, then you can try to expand to new and bigger aspects of his dysfunctional personality.

> **Boss:** You have an ugly task ahead of you.
>
> **You:** That's because I'm sitting across the table from you. Ha ha!

Your boss will think this good-natured ribbing is a sign that he's bonding with you. Bosses are funny that way. Using a version of weasel creep, you can continue to escalate the abuse.

> **Boss:** Do you have those numbers I asked for?
>
> **You:** No, you miserable piece of $#*!! Ha ha!

Continue making your jokes until you get a look from your boss that is like this one . . .

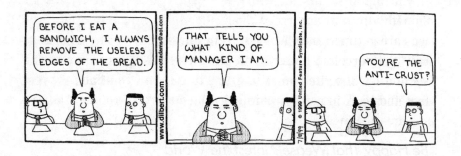

27

Final Thoughts on Weasels

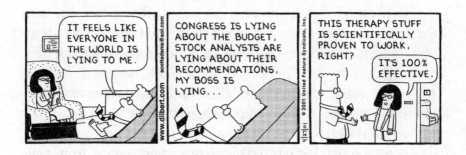

If you made it this far into the book, you're probably disillusioned with humanity to the point of despair. And perhaps your legs are getting numb from sitting on what the Native Americans call "the porcelain library with one seat." But don't worry. In this section I will write something uplifting to get you back on your feet and back in a chipper mood.

Be Happy That Weasels Infest the World

Weasels are like motor oil for society. It wouldn't be fair to judge motor oil outside the context of the engine. If you put motor oil in your mouth, it would be slimy and filthy and leave a bad taste.

But when that oil is inside an engine, it does an important job and you're glad it's there. Weasels are the same way: slimy and disgusting but essential. And you don't want them in your mouth.

Without weasels there would be no romance, no government, no friendship, and no commerce. Every once in a while I get a glimpse of what the world would be like with no weasels, and frankly it's frightening. For example, the other day a friend saw someone at her church who she said *looked exactly like* me. She went on to describe the similarities, including my freakish tuft of hair that stands up like an angry rooster around the perimeter of my bald spot. My churchy double had the same tragic hair-thing, which raises all sorts of questions about the power of prayer. But that's another book.

My point is that I didn't want to hear that my twin has freakish hair. I wanted to hear that he was "almost as sexy" as I am. I wanted the courtesy of being weaseled.

And when it comes to money, I *need* to be weaseled. For example, take buying a car. Who would pay for a car if they knew in advance the shellacking they were going to get? I don't want to know how badly I'm getting reamed. I prefer to pay dearly for invisible rust protection, $500 floor mats, and a warranty against things that don't even exist. I don't want to hear the truth—that "sometimes this model blows up." In fact, I'll pay *extra* to avoid that sort of knowledge. Just weasel me and give me my car, please. Weasels provide me with the false sense of certainty I need to make decisions. Without that, I'd be walking everywhere, probably naked and hungry.

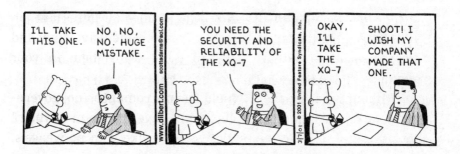

The point is, if we allow ourselves to be bamboozled regularly, it stimulates the economy and creates disposable income for weasels who are then able to buy whatever defective products *we're* selling.

And that reminds me: thank you for reading my book.*

Weasel Immortality

Weaseling has more than short-term benefits. I plan to use weasel techniques to be immortal. They say you can't take your money with you when you die. But they're wrong. I have a plan to do just that. I'm going to have myself cloned and leave all my money to my clone, except for a trust fund for whoever wants to raise the little monstrosity. All of this will happen after the original version of me dies. There's some risk that the clone will turn out to look like Keith Richards, and that would be a tragedy. But

*The sequel is already in bookstores. It *looks* exactly like this book but the words are pronounced differently.

knowing me, my clone will do something later to deserve that sort of punishment, so it's fair.

My clone won't be born with my memories, but I consider that a plus. I'll tell him what he needs to know in an instructional video that I'll leave behind. I'll leave out all the unpleasant memories. And I'll include tips on how to maximize the body I know so well.

Tips for my clone:

- Spend *less* time at football practice and *more* time learning to draw.

- Hit the Rogaine early.

- Use self-tanning gel on your legs so you don't scare people.

- Just say no to cubicles.

You could argue that my clone isn't really me. But the way I look at it, *I'm* not me anymore either. I don't have any of the same cells I was born with. They've all been replaced several times. The only thing I have in common with my younger me is the pattern of my DNA and some false memories. My clone will have all of that, plus—thanks to improvements in nutrition—he'll be four inches taller and cavity-free. He'll have enough cash to get a nice car in high school and—because of that automotive advantage—get to second base with a cheerleader for the first time ever. (I'm persistent.)

I realize cloning isn't foolproof yet, so I'll try to stay alive as long as possible. People say I won't enjoy being over a hundred years old because the quality of life will be bad. But I'm counting on the medical community to invent some prescription drugs that are the next level better than Prozac and Paxil and Viagra. The existing drugs are a good start, but they don't go far enough. It's great that people can take a pill to feel less depressed or less shy or to boost their sexual staying power, but I want more. When I'm 130 years old, I want a pill that makes me so happy and so unself-conscious and so randy I'm willing to make love to my fuzzy bed slippers on my front lawn and yodel at the same time. And I want it to last all night.

And I hope replacement body parts are better by then. I don't want a new hip that's only "just as good" as the one I had. I want new powers. I want to be able to leap from the three-point line and dunk a basketball. And forget about giving me some stinkin' pig heart if my original equipment stops ticking. I want a titanium heart that doubles as an MP3 player.

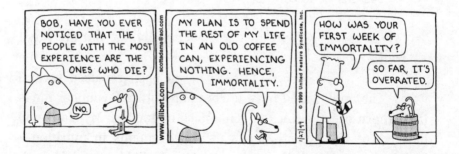

Overall, I'm quite optimistic about a weasel-filled future. You should be too. And feel free to follow my blueprint for immortality through cloning. Our clones can hang out together and maybe form a start-up company. But don't be surprised if one of the clones gets disgruntled and quits the company to draw comics about it.

That's all the wisdom I have for now. If I think of anything else, I'll call you at home.

Comments are always welcome.

E-mail: scottadams@aol.com

About the Author

Scott Adams is the creator of Dilbert, the comic strip that now appears in more than 2,000 newspapers, sixty-five countries, and twenty-two languages. His books, *The Dilbert Principle, Dogbert's Top Secret Management Handbook, The Joy of Work,* and *The Dilbert Future,* were all *New York Times* bestsellers.